THE PHOTOGRAPHY WORKSHOP SERIES

Todd Hido

on Landscapes, Interiors, and the Nude

**Introduction
by Gregory Halpern**

aperture

Table of Contents

Introduction

By Gregory Halpern

I took several semester-long classes with Todd Hido when
I was in graduate school at California College of the Arts
and I would meet with him to show my work in-progress,
sometimes at his home—an old Craftsman house with lovely,
wooden details, filled with all things photographic. Framed
prints sat next to weathered postcards; pin-up pictures from
the 1940s were propped against vintage vases filled with
flowers, and the dining room table was always overflowing
with photobooks. It was thrilling to see first-hand how a
working artist created a space, a life. Often Todd had one
book open next to a spread from another. There were little
piles everywhere, which were almost sculptural, made of
ephemera, found images, signs, or newspaper clippings. It
was great when Todd went into the kitchen or took a phone
call for a few minutes, so I could poke around, randomly
open books, and study the beautifully organized maelstrom
of images.

At our first meeting, Todd told me, "The first thing you
need to do is buy a car." I was carless at the time, and my work
involved a certain amount of urban meandering. He convinced
me I couldn't do it all on foot. He also convinced me to buy
the old Acura he happened to be selling! This was classic Todd
—always the practical businessman ready to make a deal,
but also generous and right. He gave me a bargain price, and
my work improved greatly with that car.

As a mentor, Todd was straightforward and unpretentious.
His influences were more visual and personal (from pulp fiction
novels to childhood memories to BMX racing), than they
were intellectual, which I found refreshing in an academic
environment. He told me it was possible to make it as an artist.
It was hard, he said, but not impossible. This simple bit of
encouragement went a long way. Most of all, Todd loved photography, cameras, film, prints, and the darkroom. His love of
photography and beauty felt old-fashioned and wonderful.

Whenever I was struggling with something, it seemed like
Todd always had the right practical advice. "When you're
printing something in a subjective way," he might say, "make

contact sheets in three totally different color palettes so you can see what it might look like." And in life, too, Todd was full of great advice: "You can't get sucked into e-mail," he told me one day. "Think of it like the batting cage—you've got a few minutes to get in as many hits as you can." I had chosen to attend CCA primarily because I wanted to study photobooks, and along with Todd, CCA's faculty included Larry Sultan and Jim Goldberg, whose books I had admired for years. I learned a lot from considering my teachers' feedback in relation to their work, and Todd was no exception to this. His second book, *Outskirts*, had just come out, and I spent a lot of time looking at it, as well as his first book, *House Hunting*. Those books were both short, and I wondered how they felt so complete and powerful with so few images. I wanted to know how he edited and asked him about his process one day. He smiled and said without missing a beat, "All killer; no filler." I still hear those words whenever I edit.

His work ethic was legendary. He never said "work harder." I just always saw him working, so I worked harder. The best was if you could manage to print in the color (analog) darkroom on the days when Todd printed. He often did so late, and sometimes we would be there into the wee hours. Once, when he was leaving the darkroom, and I was proud to be printing still, he said, "Don't print 'til 4:00 a.m. Stop at midnight and get some sleep. I'm going home now so I'll have more energy to come back and print tomorrow."

While waiting for my own color prints, I would watch his luscious landscapes pour out of the machine. Seeing our prints next to each other on the magnetic board, it was hard to believe they were printed on the same equipment. Nonetheless, Todd would pay my work an occasional compliment, keeping the wind in my sails. Years later, after I began teaching, he told me that it was important to always find something to be encouraging about in a student's work. I always remember this in the classroom.

I am often struck that someone as successful as Todd can also be as generous. Artists can guard their secrets, but Todd doesn't hoard his. He really wants all of us to succeed. Much of that spirit and that advice is here in this book.

A Reason to Press the Shutter

I'm not a person who can just go and photograph anything. I've never been a street or documentary photographer, where the whole world is out there to be discovered and photographed. That's never compelled me. There has to be something that pulls me in; I have to have a reason to press the shutter. I think that there's something essential about the impulse to record something; I don't take pictures just to take pictures. There has to be something about a place or a person that I recognize, that I need to record or remember or think about again.

The primary thing that draws me in is when I see something that reminds me of places that I've been before, that remind me of where I grew up in Ohio. Since I left home after high school, I've always been trying to find it again in some way. I looked at a map of my old neighborhood one day, just to look again at where I came from, and realized that almost everything on the map appeared in my work in some way.

Sometimes, it's important to explore the world that's right in front of you, but at other times, you need to travel and get away from your life in order to recognize it. For me, I keep finding and exploring the same place no matter where I go. I draw from within, from my own history, as the basis of my work. All of the memories and experiences from my past come together subconsciously and form a kind of fragmented narrative.

In this book, I'll discuss some of the struggles and triumphs I've experienced in my career while giving practical, professional, and creative advice along the way. The book starts with me talking about my early work and influences and then moves into an exploration of how I approach exteriors (night photography and landscape) and from there, interiors (rooms and people). Ultimately, I follow these different paths to address how photos speak to a viewer and to each other, reflecting on ideas of narrative in photography and ways to pull your work together in books or exhibitions.

I'll give you my best advice here up-front: Measure twice, cut once. And if you ever pass something that you think you might want to photograph and say to yourself, "I'll go back later and get that," stop now and photograph it, because you'll never get back there, or if you do, it won't be the same. You've got to take the photograph right away, when the impulse is there. Use whatever camera that you have with you, even if it's only your phone.

This doesn't mean don't work to get a good picture. A lot of people think, "I'll fix it in Photoshop, or I'll fix it in post." You'll be ten times better as a photographer if you don't rely on those things. It's nice and handy that these tools exist, and it's true that you could fix the picture in Photoshop. However, I believe that we should all strive to get it right in the camera.

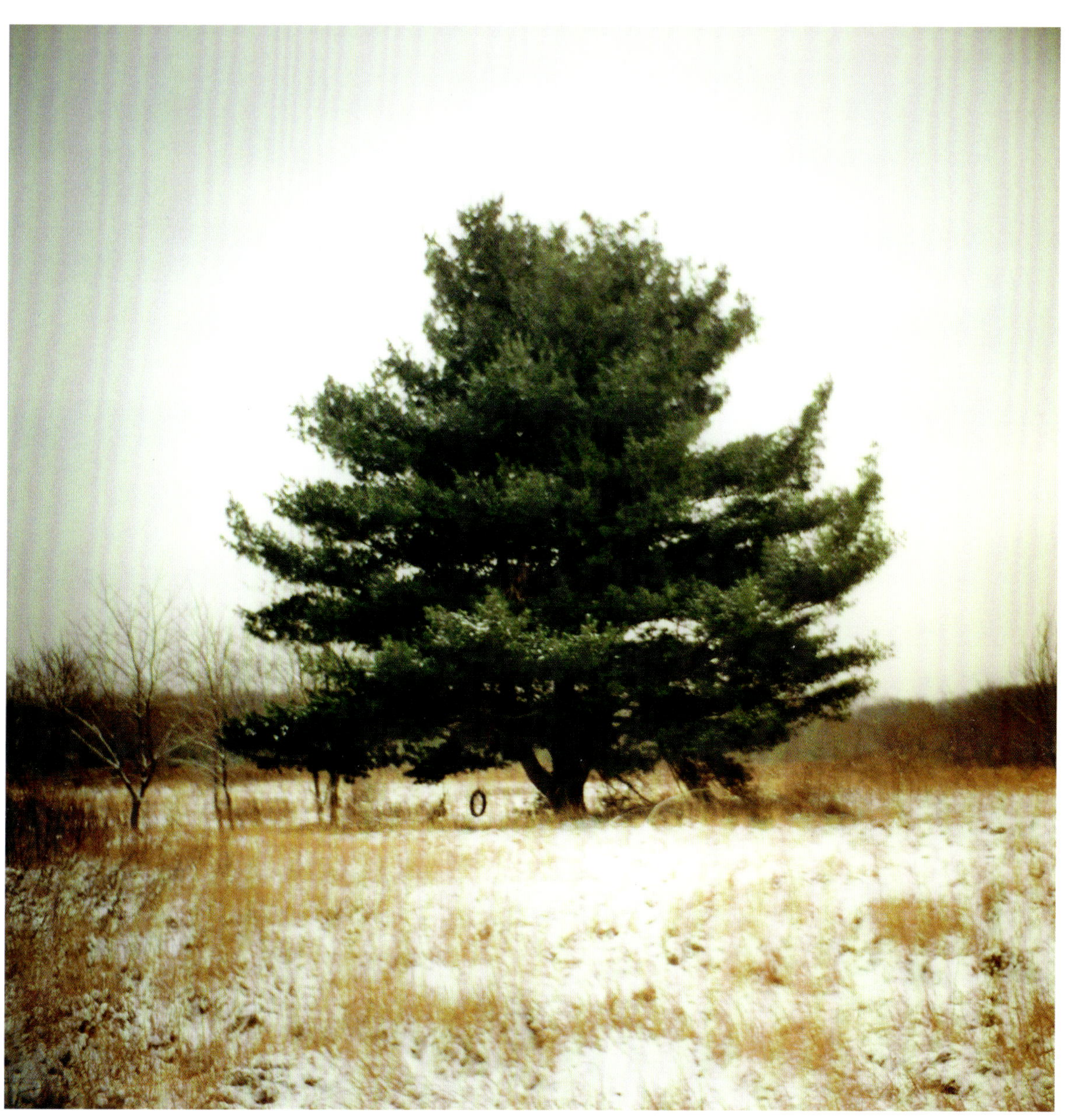

Todd Hido
#9238-a

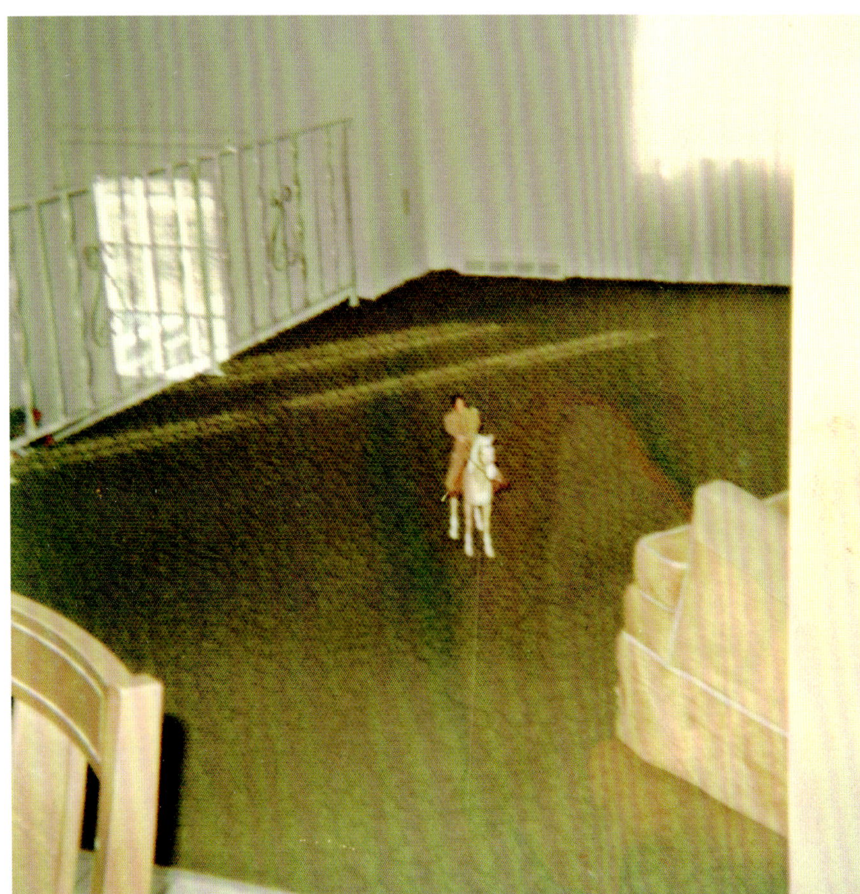

I grew up in a suburban development that was built into the cornfields, very much like the kind of place you would see in Robert Adams's work. Though it was a suburban place, it was also very rural. Our neighborhood was called Silver Meadows, but the nickname was Silver Ghettos. There were these apartment buildings next to us. They were almost like the projects. And my mom would always say, "You can do anything you want, just don't go to the apartments." Of course, we hung out there all the time. If we weren't in the woods, we were in the apartments.

My babysitter's name was Marilyn Monroe. She lived two houses down. She was strict. She made me drink my broth, or I couldn't get up from the table.

My father was a plumber, and my mom worked at a drugstore. She used to get those 126 film cartridges and give them to me. So the first camera I had was a 126 Kodak, an Instamatic camera. This is one of my first pictures: our living room.

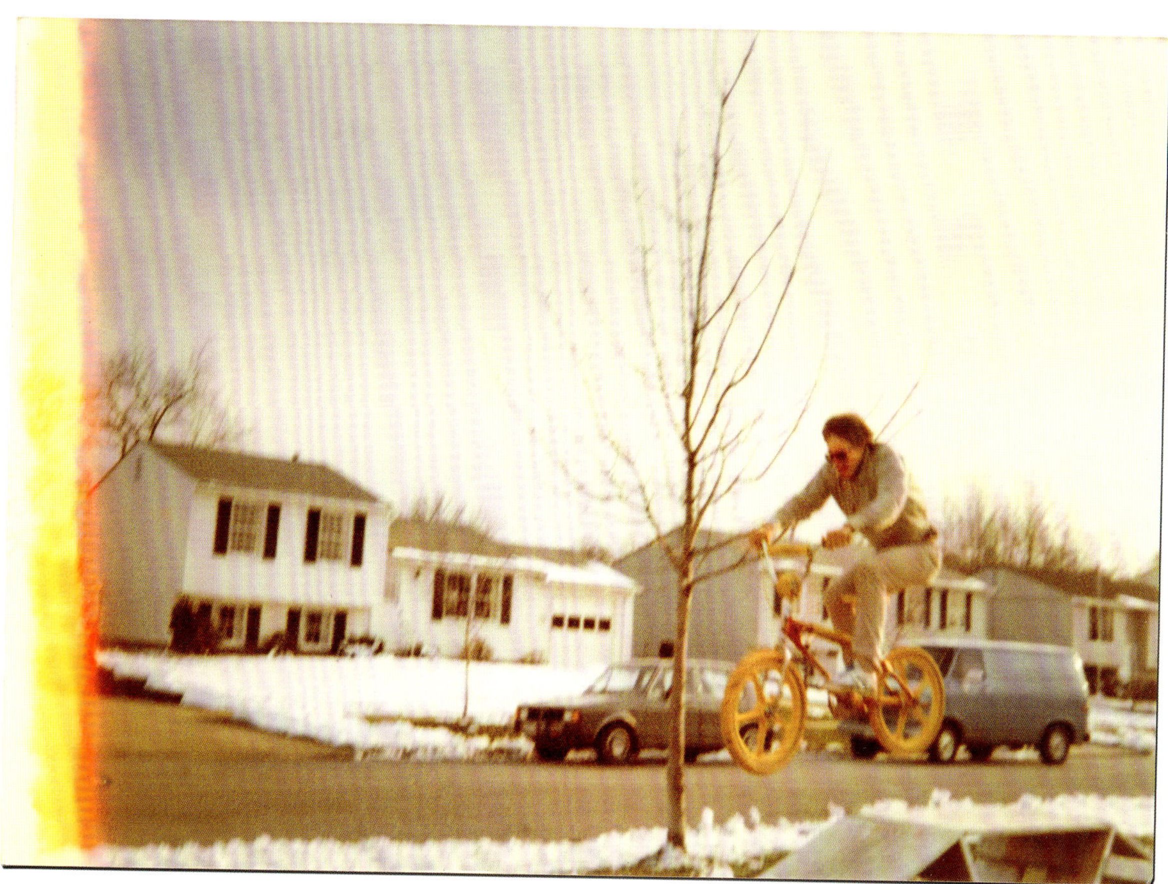

I was the state champion in Ohio for BMX racing. Though I liked taking snapshots as a kid, this is when I really picked up the camera—to photograph my friends racing and jumping. We set up ramps, and I would take pictures of my brother jumping them. That was my real introduction to photography, trying to capture the drama of jumps in mid-air that only lasted a fleeting few moments. I'm also drawn to an open horizon, which reminds me of those flat roads I'd ride my bike on in Ohio. I remember thinking that I was going to move to California and become a BMX photographer. I got there in other ways I suppose. Once I got my driver's license I moved on from bicycles to cars.

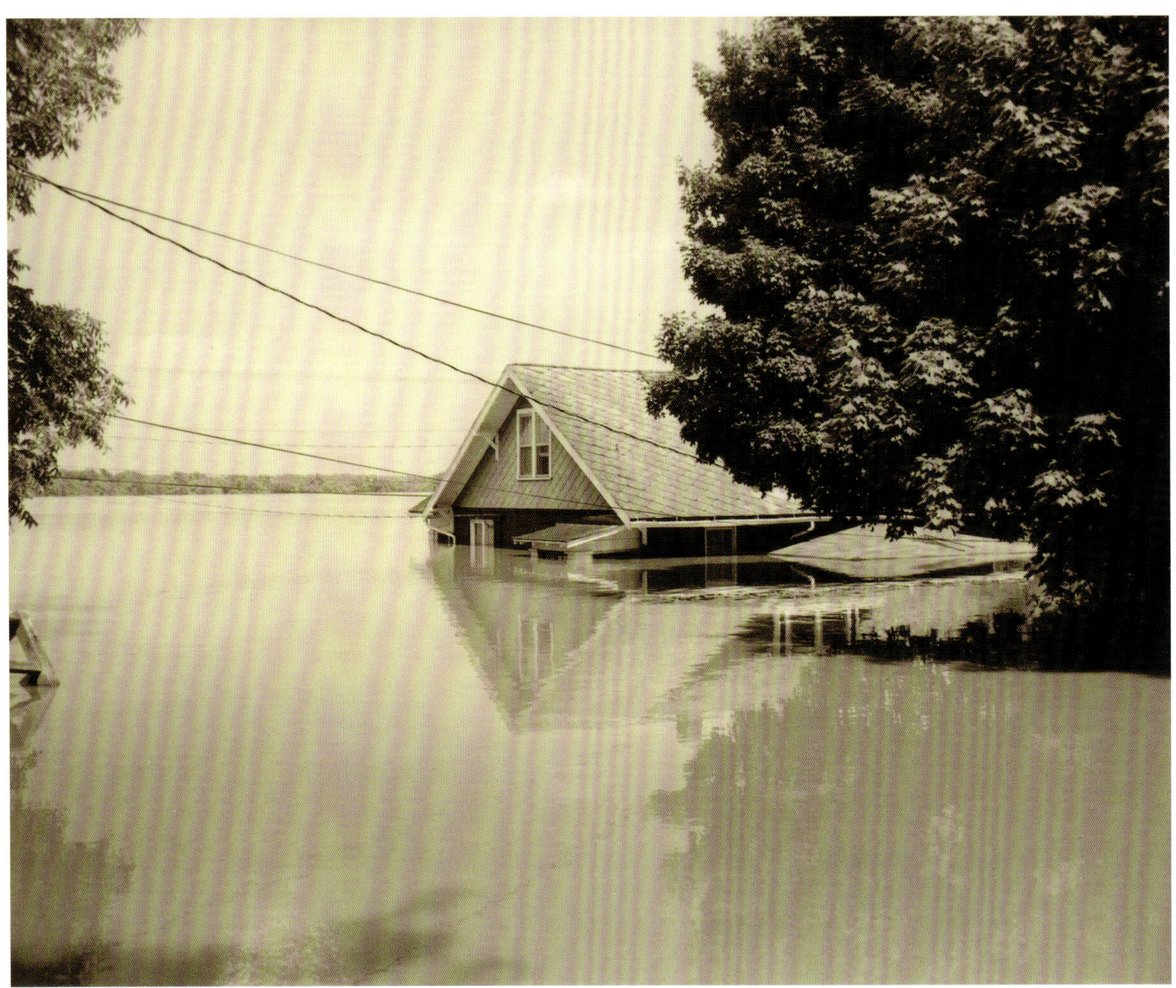

Early on in my photographic education, at a time when I wanted to be just like Emmet Gowin and was photographing my girlfriend in black and white, I saw a show at the Museum of Modern Art in New York called *The Pleasures and Terrors of Domestic Comfort*. It was an amazing exhibit about home and family. Many of the photographs showed people at home, but they were not always at ease. The pictures didn't present a sentimental or warm-hearted view of home. They were more ambiguous— at times funny or affectionate or unsettling. That was the crucial thing I saw in the show. I thought, "Wow, there's something here that really moves me." I felt like I had something to say that was similar; I didn't grow up in the most stable home.

Larry Sultan was in that show with his work about his parents, Pictures from Home. I really liked how he used the home as a set for small family dramas, those that reveal larger and more complex longings, complications, insecurities, intimacy, and alienation. At that time, I was applying to graduate schools and really wanted to go to the University of New Mexico, which was the cool place to go. That was my first choice, but I didn't get in. I had applied to California College of the Arts, too, not even realizing that Larry Sultan taught there. I ended up there instead. Imagine if I had gotten in to UNM? My life would be completely different. I never would have met Larry Sultan.

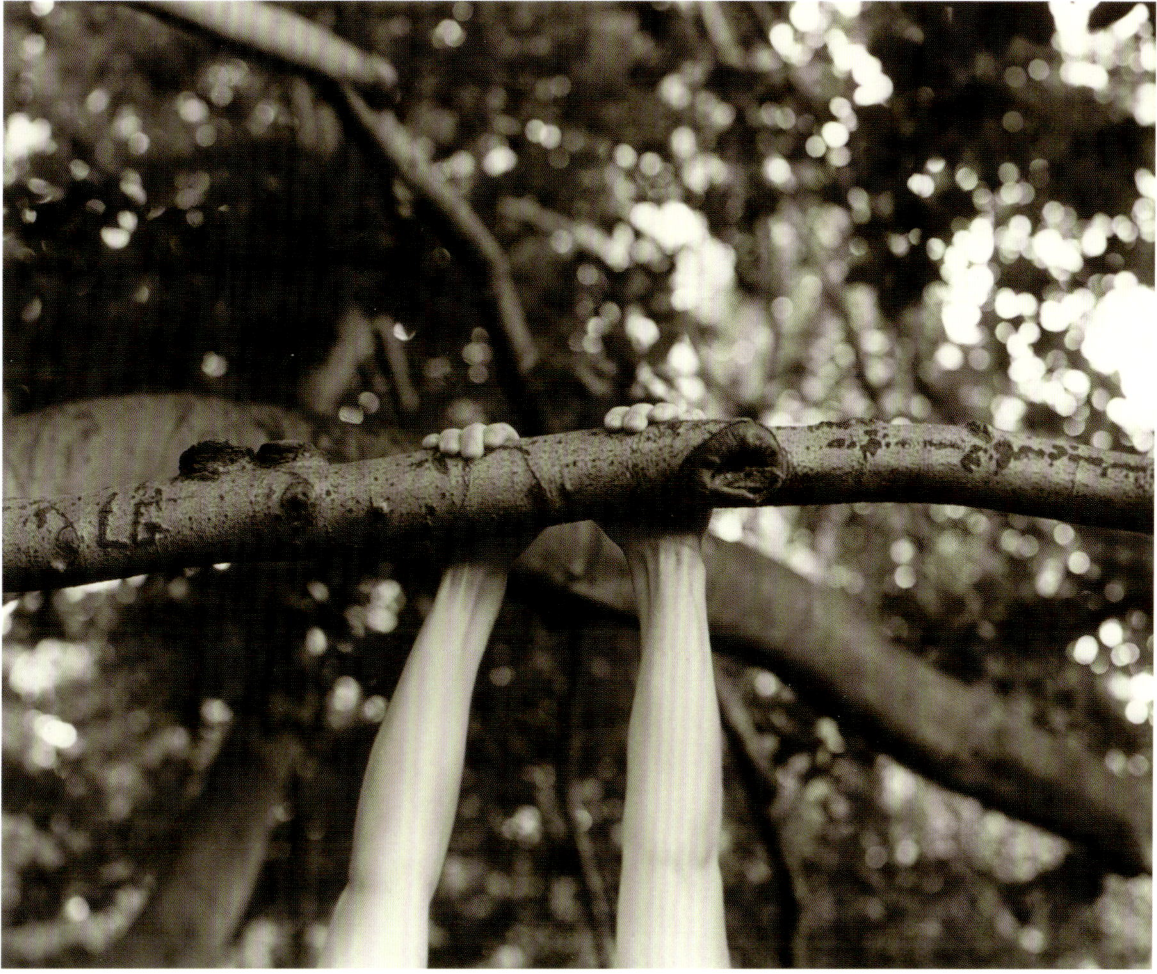

In the first days of graduate school, we were presenting our work, and I remember how Larry noticed the picture above immediately. He was touched by the strain in the hands. He recognized something there and said, "That picture's about the human condition and not about somebody in a tree. It's emotional." That's one of the most important things I learned from Larry; he made it okay to make pictures that were emotional, and it was really important for me to open that door.

Some people go to graduate school to get themselves organized and to professionalize their practice. I wanted to use the time in grad school to change up my work, to see what else I could do, to make different pictures than I had in the past.

One of our first assignments was the "alter ego" assignment, where you have to become another artist and make his or her work instead of your own. This is a great assignment since it frees you to try on different ideas. It is a chance to do or be anything you want, to recognize that you're not married to your past or the path you're on. Night photography, for me, evolved out of this assignment.

Seeing in the Dark

I'm a wandering photographer. I just go out, usually by car, and shoot. I know that if I go out looking, I will find something.

I arrive at most things in my work through a series of accidents and coincidences. I didn't set out to do a night shot. I was just out shooting, and I didn't want my day of making pictures to be over. As it got dark, I kept shooting.

Shooting in a new and different situation, like the dark, doesn't have to be complicated or anxiety-ridden, especially these days when your phone can make a picture of most situations, even when there's no light. I just exposed the film for longer, and the pictures turned out. And I turned the camera around and photographed what was behind me.

When I saw this picture of a house at night lit up by a neighbor's floodlight, I realized that night photography was something I wanted to explore more. Even though this picture was taken in 1997, it could have been made in 1977 because of the look of the van and the style of the house. I was also struck by how the fog changes the picture. The atmosphere is moody and melancholy. I accidentally stumbled upon these elements, and it was like being transported into another world.

Todd Hido
#2122

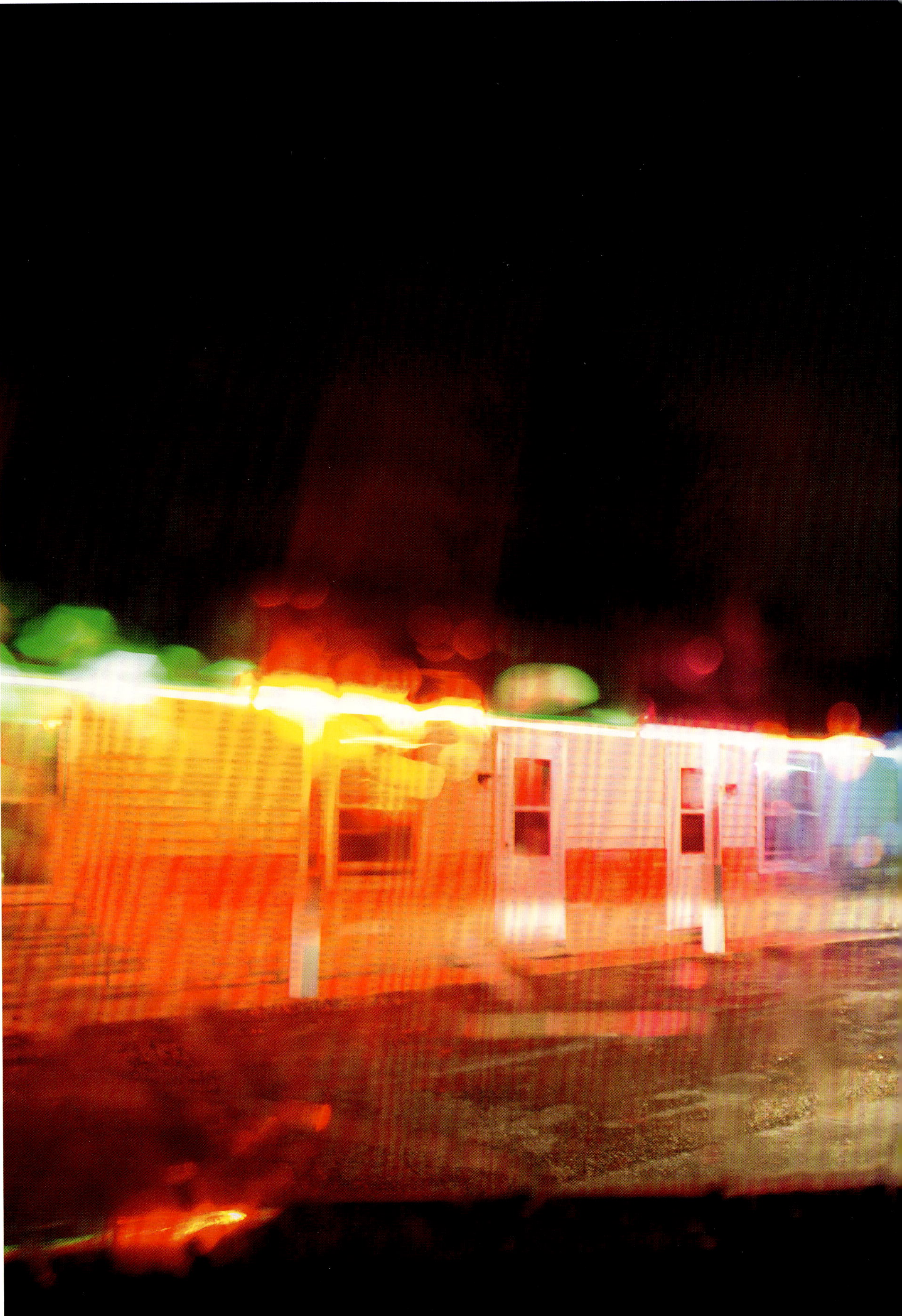

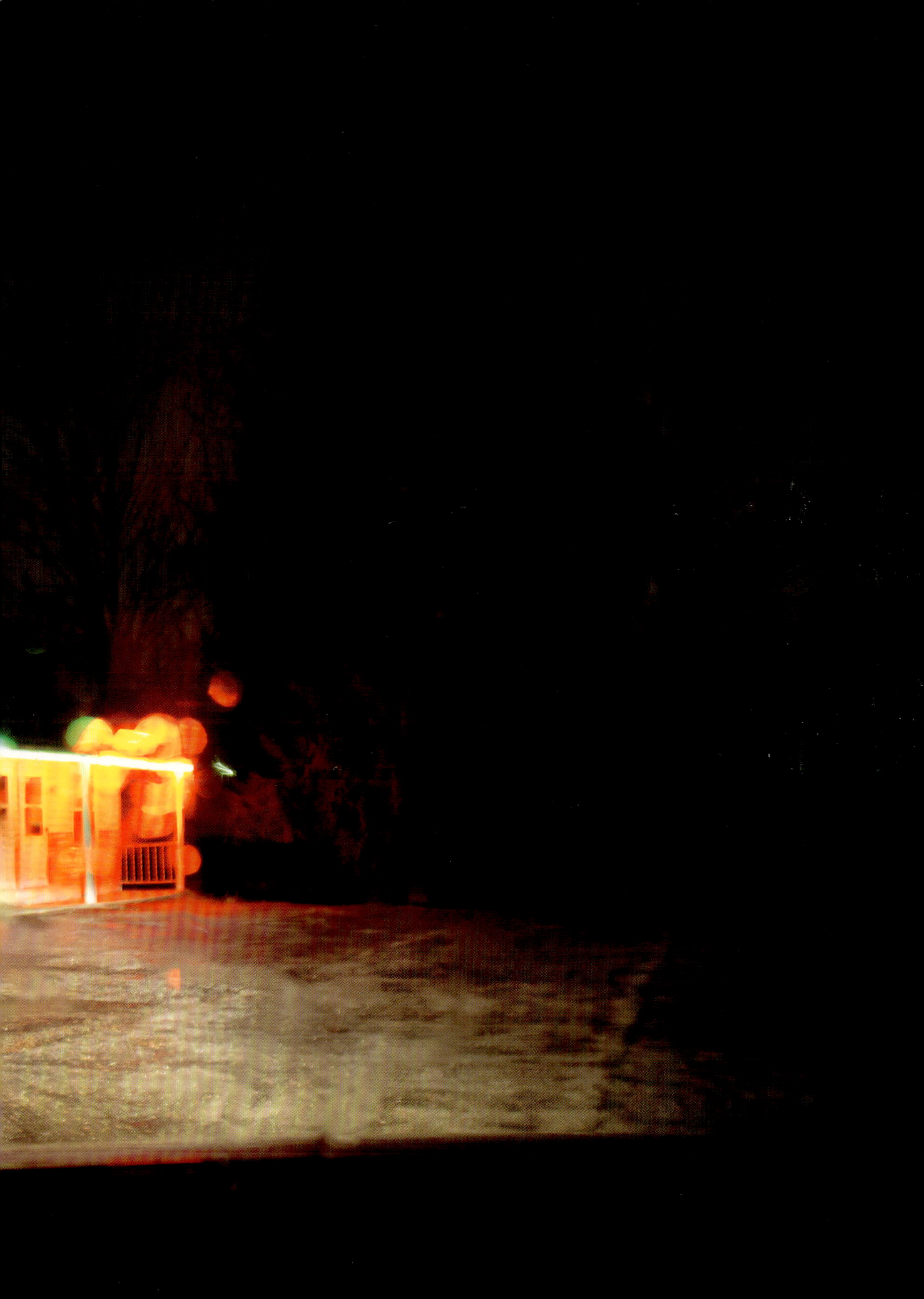

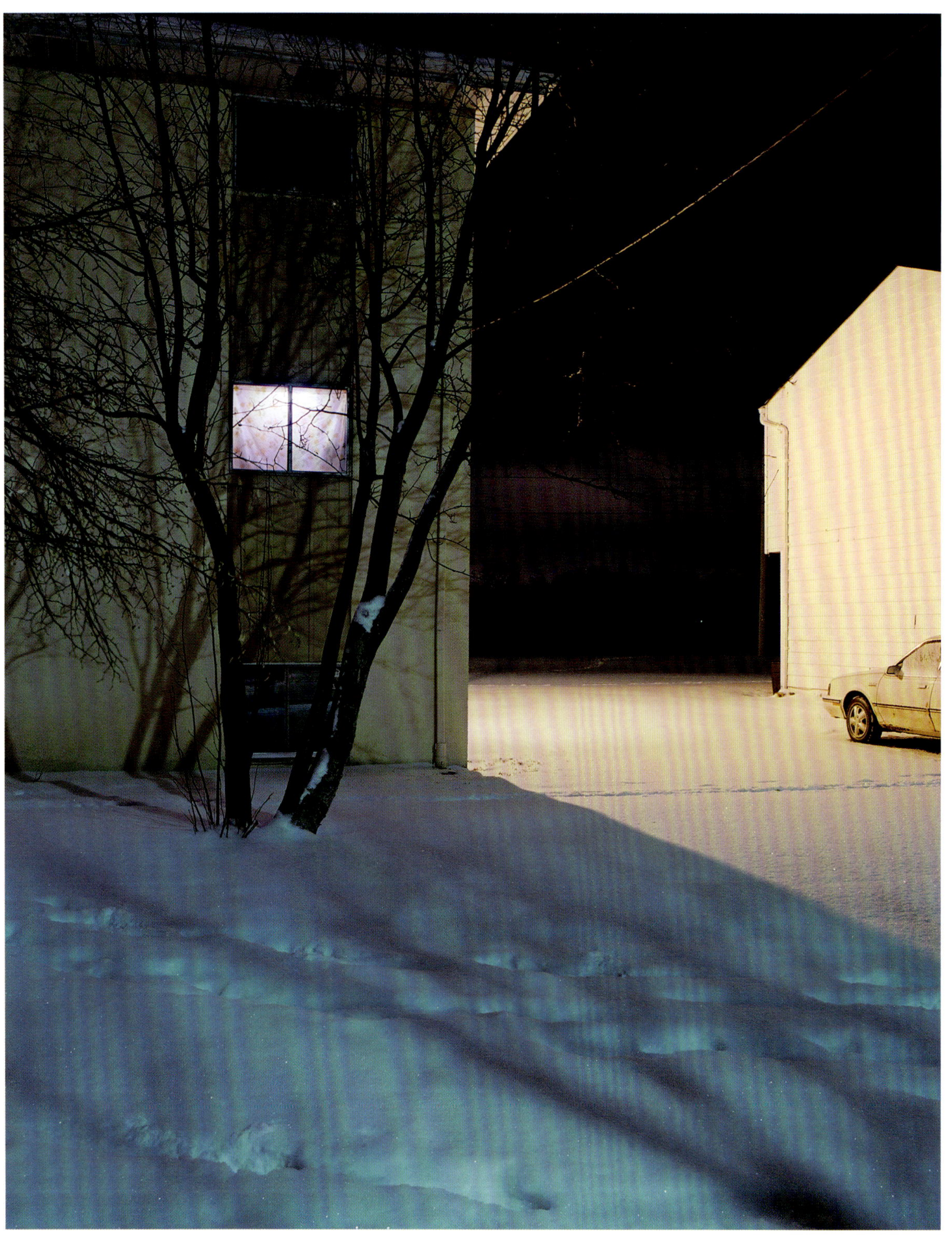

I see differently in the dark. Night is a quiet time without as much going on. The world moves slower. Lots of things disappear into the darkness.

You might not notice this about my work at first, but I'm a minimalist. I like for the frame to be neat and organized. At night, most of the frame is black, and that just works for me aesthetically. All of that darkness and negative space helps to focus and isolate the subject. It brings me (and the viewer) right to the subject.

Most of the time, I am interested in a certain light in a window—that's what catches my attention. When you're looking at a house at night with its lights on, you can't help but imagine the people inside. The inside literally seeps into the outside through that light. Perhaps because I had a traumatic childhood, I've always looked at people's houses and wondered what goes on in there. Is it like what happened at my house? In a strange way, I'm making a picture of a place that's actually about people.

Almost as soon as I made my first picture of a house with a lit-up window, I recognized that this was not about the house. This was about psychology and relationships.

Pages 16–17
Todd Hido
#10789-2109

Left
Todd Hido
#2840

Where Do You Stand?

When I made the picture on the cover of my *House Hunting* book, I had driven around for five or six hours that night and shot nothing. I was ready to go home, but then I turned the corner and saw this house. I knew it was exactly what I wanted.

I shot a number of pictures. You can see where I started on the bottom left of the contact sheet; I'm standing very far away. I moved around to figure out the distance, and in this particular case, the best vantage point was closer to the house. You can see that I initially circled a different frame. I needed to look at the contact sheet several times and wait for some time to pass before I recognized that the shot in the corner was more emotional. You feel like you're peeking right over the fence. You also know you're on the outside because the fence is the line that divides the viewer from the house and the property. I've often thought about Paul Strand's iconic image, *The White Fence*—how he used the fence to create both a dynamic composition and also to say something larger about American society.

Emmet Gowin once said to me, "photography is about position." I use this diagonal perspective a lot. There's a vanishing point or a corner. In fact, I think there's only one photograph I've made of a building that is shot straight on like a Walker Evans. When photographing space, it is useful to use perspective to draw the viewer into the frame. The diagonal line creates depth, and depth often works well in describing an environment. The diagonal lines extend your photograph into infinity somehow.

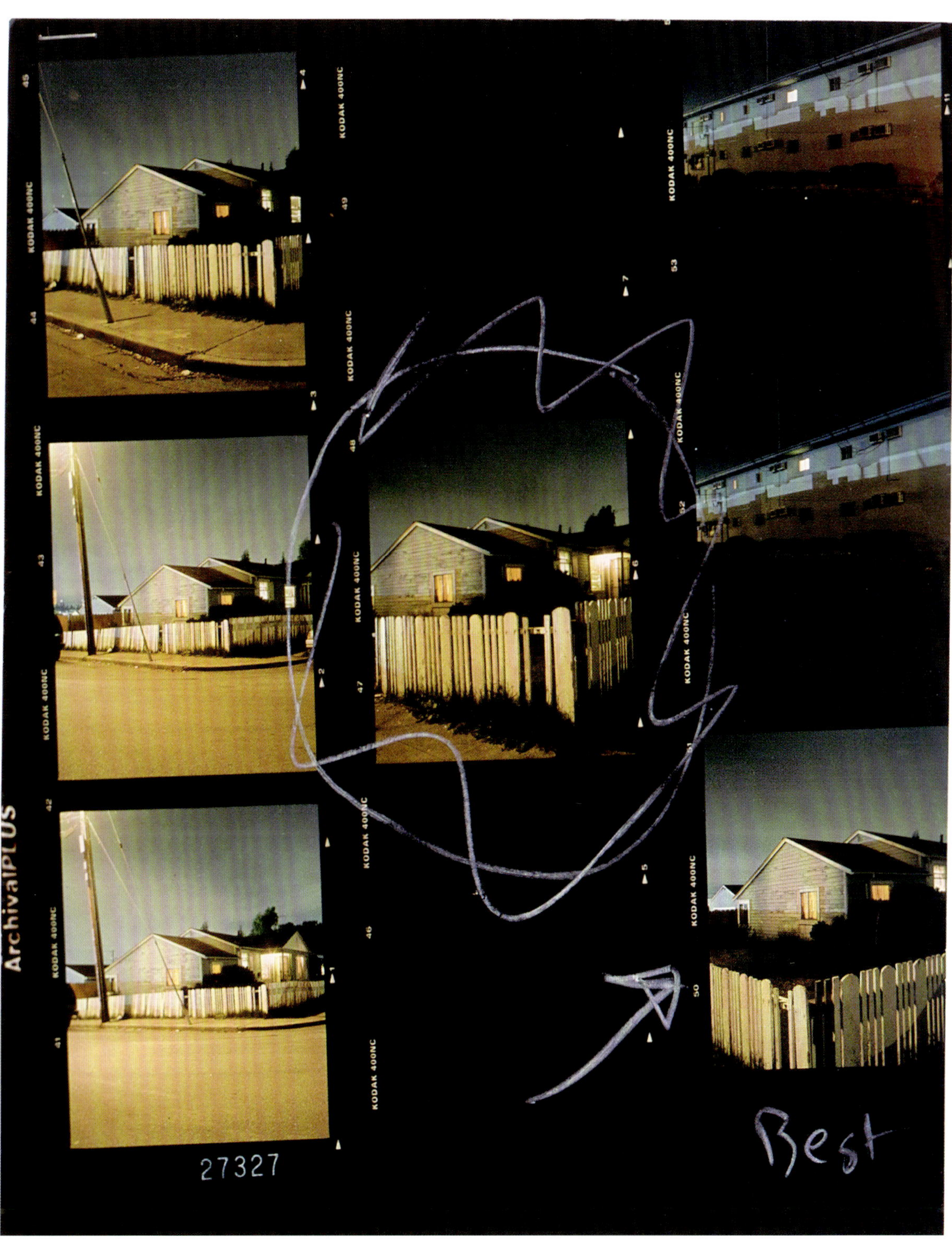

Todd Hido
Contact sheet of #2690

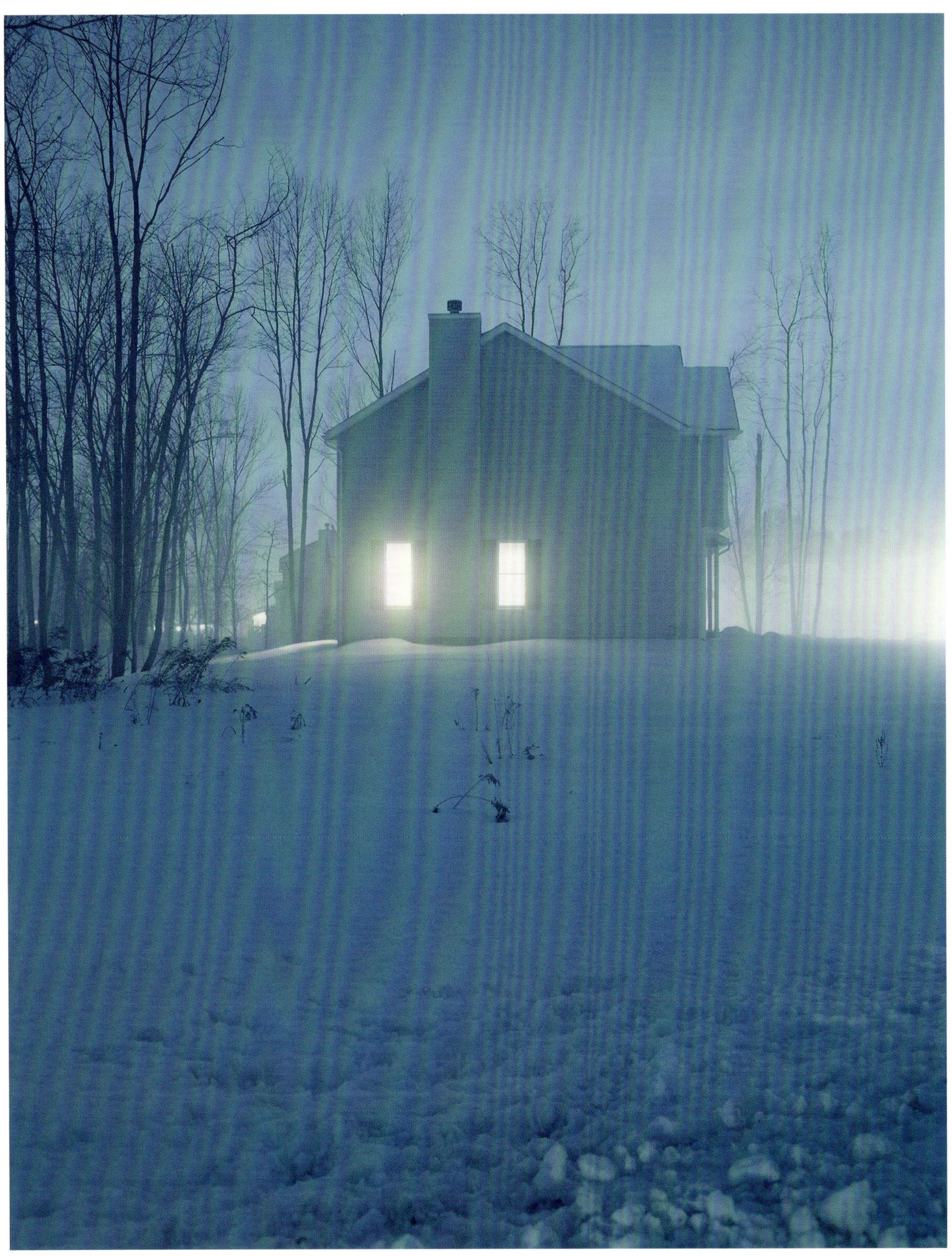

Todd Hido
#2423-a

People sometimes describe my work as voyeuristic. Where I'm standing with the camera feels voyeuristic. I'm backed up far enough away so that we (I and the viewer) are decidedly at a distance from the house. We're back across the street, on the sidewalk—a safe looking distance. Maybe we're not too close because we're not supposed to be there. I've always used this odd distance that communicates, "I'm not from there." Viewers feel that distance and actually become more aware of my presence as a photographer/voyeur. I place them in the same position—a position that encourages a certain type of looking.

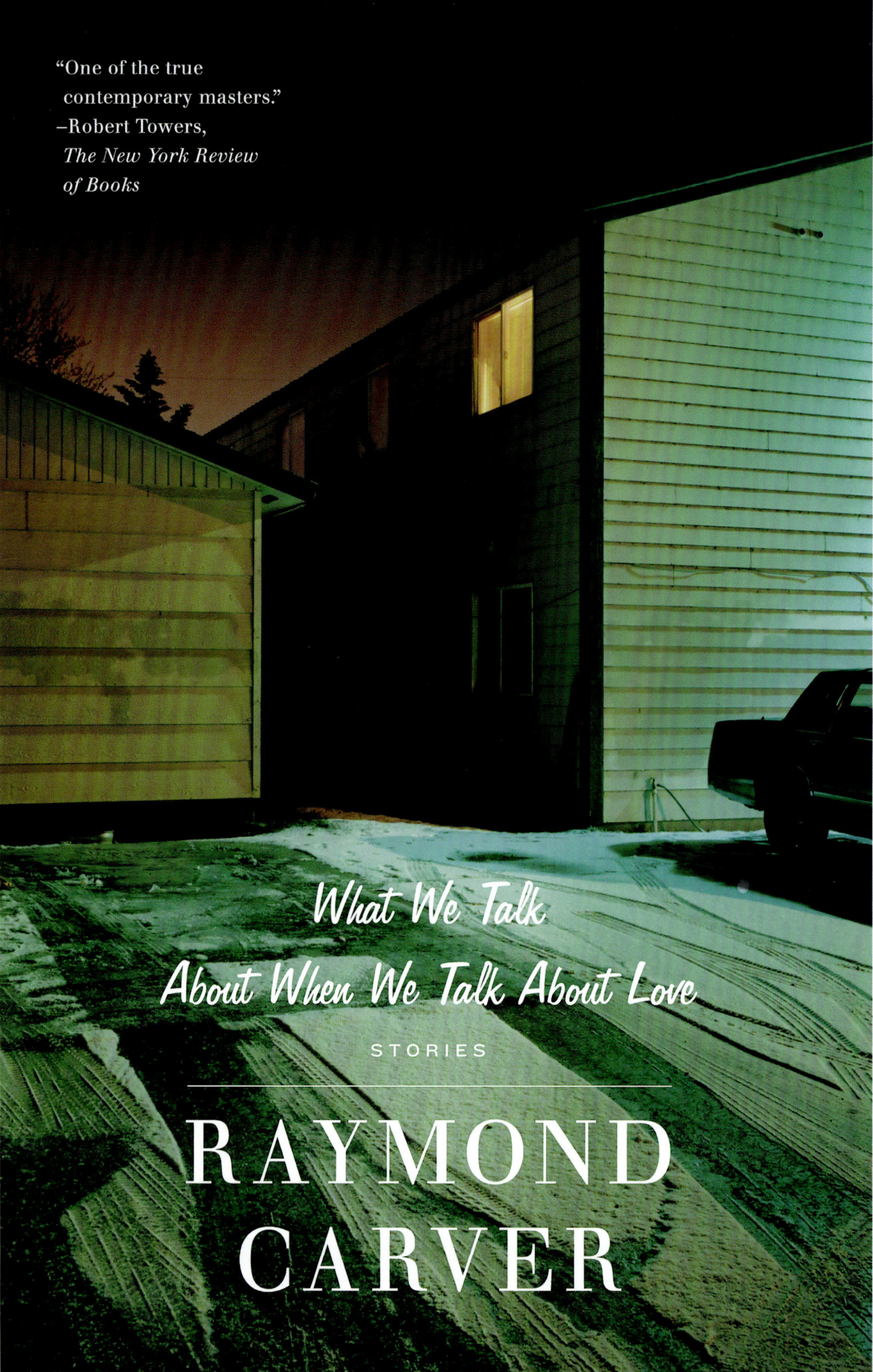

"One of the true contemporary masters."
—Robert Towers,
The New York Review of Books
What We Talk About When We Talk About Love
STORIES
RAYMOND CARVER

The Drama in Details

The way people present themselves to the world says a lot about what's happening inside their home—for instance, whether their grass is cut or not. I can recognize the chaos in their curtains. How'd the curtains get all messed up? Don't they notice that they're askew? They don't fix the curtains because they can't see them as betraying secrets about the home. You're blind to your own space. But others can see it, and the camera can bring it to light as well. Surface details reveal deeper stories. In a way, all photography does this because photographs only show the surface. These pictures pay attention to what is visible and hint at what is not visible, the subtle psychology of the space. Part of being a photographer is noticing surface details and how they represent something larger; it's like being a detective or psychologist.

I find myself drawn to places that reveal more of a story. Often when I'm photographing I go around to the back of the house; I start at the back instead of the front. The story isn't usually facing out. The story is often more apparent in the backyard where things aren't so cleaned up. That's where you find out about something or somebody. It's the backstory I'm interested in, where life presents its more unraveled self.

Raymond Carver's work has always resonated with me—how he focuses on everyday dramas and losses. I've included a few of his poems in my books. When I read his writing, I see pictures and think of all these ideas for photographs. A few years ago, his publisher was reeditioning the books and asked me if I would consider allowing them to use my pictures for the covers. I had to pretend I was only mildly interested, so I didn't end up giving them all the photos for free. But I knew it was a perfect fit. This cover is my favorite of all of them. My picture of an apartment building with a light on upstairs and tire tracks in the snow from a car pulling out of the driveway is exactly the kind of thing we talk about when we talk about love. The picture contains the ingredients of a story; it places the retreating tracks in relationship with the window and invites the viewer to pay attention and think about what might have just happened.

The Pleasures of Not Knowing

When I'm driving around the suburbs, I see them as if they were a set where dramas are unfolding all the time. I'm setting the stage for an imagined story.

I haven't shown anything actually taking place in the windows. Anything you think is happening is happening in your own imagination. The back-lit curtains simply trigger that. When I'm photographing, I start to fill in the gaps of the story in my mind even though the viewer may not sense that story in the finished picture. I exaggerate certain details in the scene to give a sense of something beyond what's seen. But I purposely leave things out so that people can bring their own stories into view, so that the meaning of the image ultimately resides with the viewer.

What I enjoy most is making images that are suggestive in this way, that have potential for being read with different meanings. I don't want the story to be entirely evident. When I don't understand what's happening, I'm more intrigued. Oftentimes what's not shown is of more interest. It activates the senses. There's a kind of pleasure in not knowing, in having to pay attention.

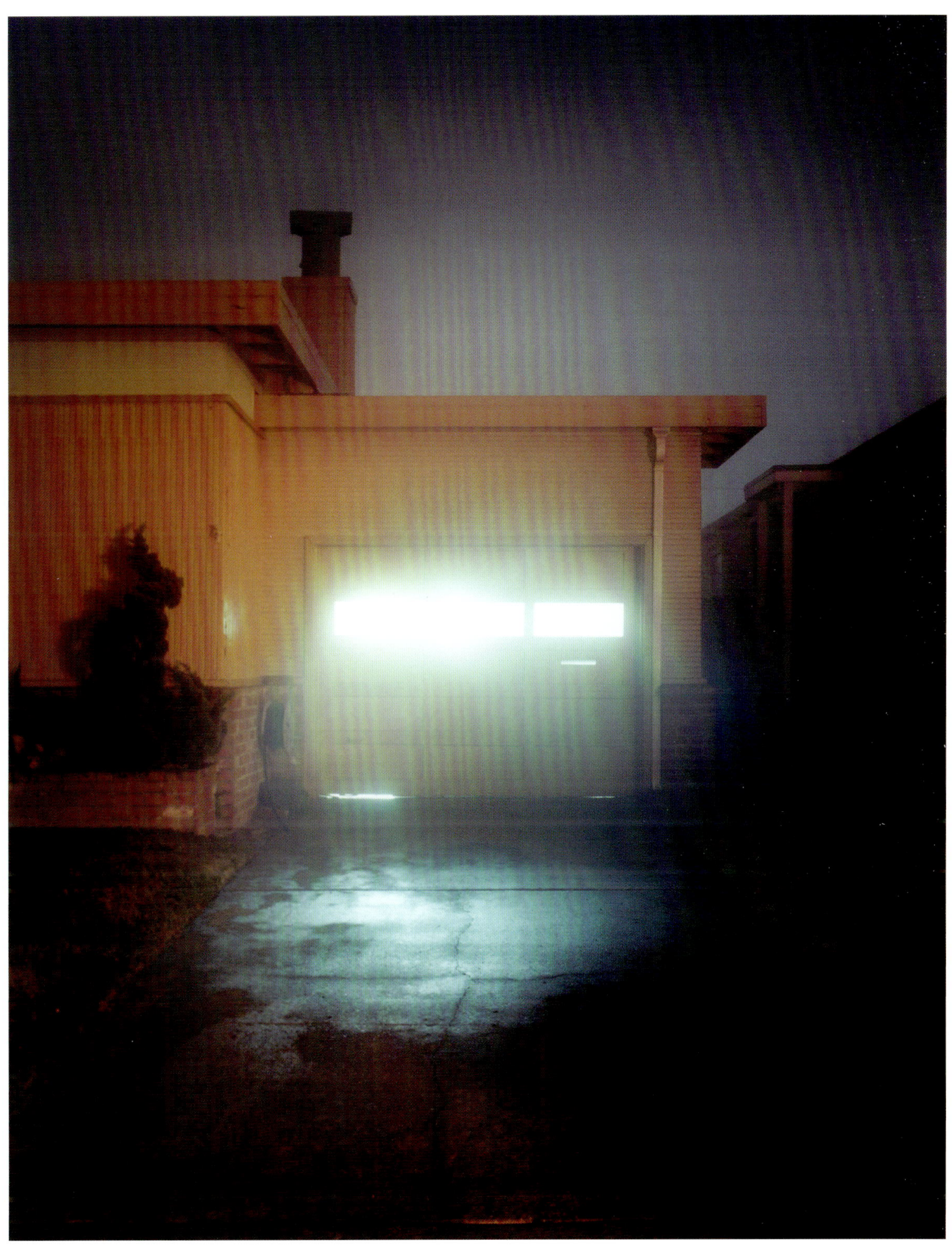

Todd Hido
#7851

**Ambiguity is one of the finest tools for making art.
In my way of thinking, images should raise more questions
than they answer.**

I want my photographs to make people wonder about what's going on instead of giving it away. I'm not necessarily saying that when work tells you something directly, it's a bad thing. But, I like when I have to ask, "What's going on here?" As a photographer, I want to tell you just enough with the pictures to activate your desire to know more.

When you look at this picture and connect the dots, you notice that both windows are lit by light from a TV. This means that there are two people watching television in the dark at night in two different rooms. When I saw this, I started to think, "Why aren't they watching TV together? Why are they sitting in separate rooms, in the dark, watching TV?" I found this sad. Maybe they don't like each other even though they live together.

Those streaks on the street are from some fool in a car making doughnuts in the middle of the intersection. It's called a "sideshow" in California. This also communicates something about the neighborhood where this house is located.

Ultimately, the camera sees more than I do. Your eyes tune into the strongest light source when you're out there at night. All the details and surprises are present in the scene, but you can't always see them in front of you while you're standing there. They emerge later when the exposure's done, like magic.

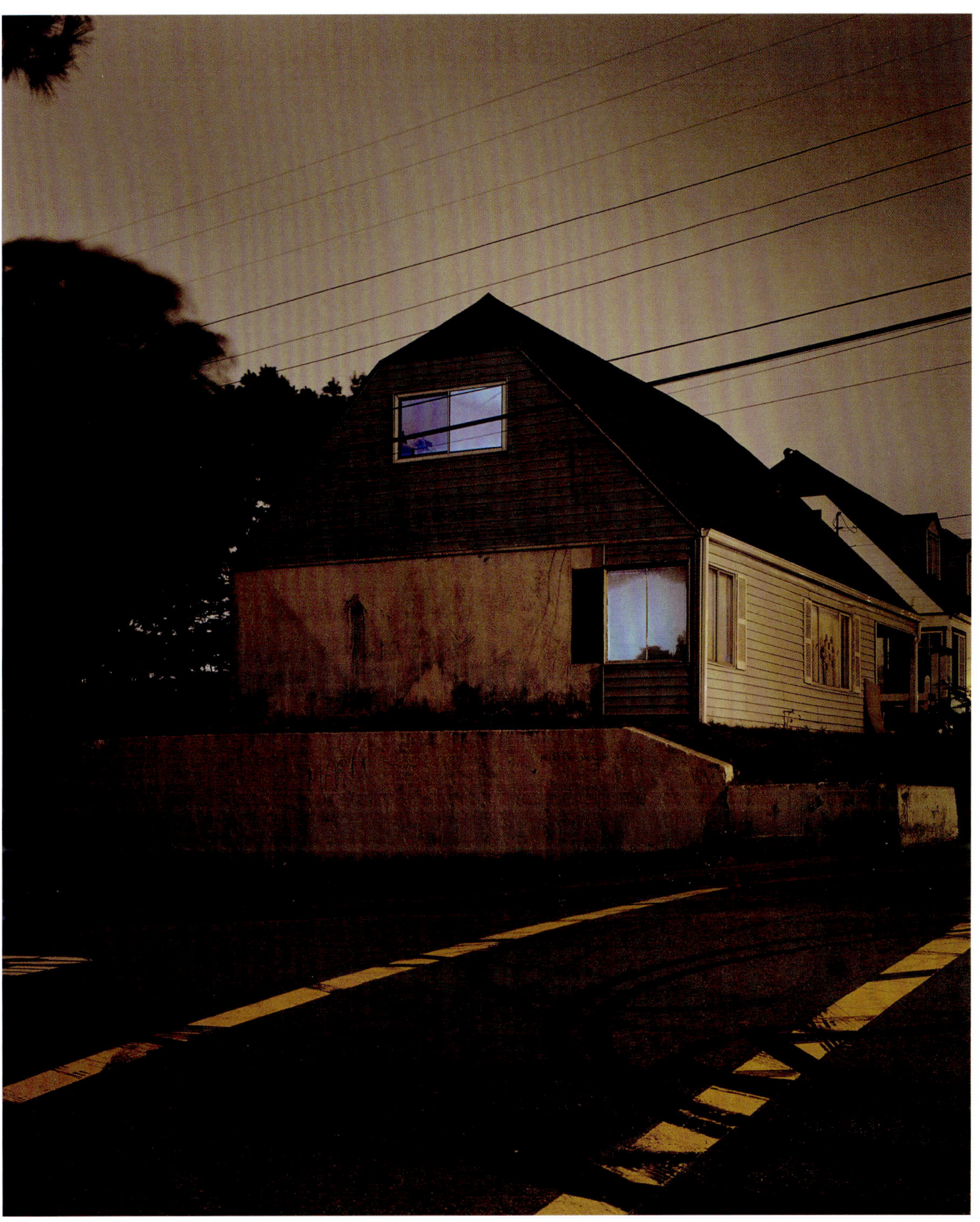

Todd Hido
#2133

29

Adding to the Conversation

As I began to realize that my pictures of houses were ultimately about relationships and home and family, I also realized that this is what makes them different from the work of those who have photographed these kind of subjects before me. My more personal take makes my work very different than that of, say, Robert Adams or Henry Wessel. The three of us would make an interesting case study because we are all photographing houses at night but yielding completely different results.

In *Summer Nights* (1985), Robert Adams photographs the same style of neighborhood that I grew up in and that I still photograph. But somehow he can photograph a house at night and I can photograph a house at night, and they're not the same thing. They almost don't even relate to each other in some odd way. Adams takes a more objective stance, while my pictures are more subjective. This goes to show that not everything has been done before. There's always room to add to the conversation.

Sometimes I have to remind myself of this. There are a million ways to talk yourself out of making your work, and saying to yourself that it's already been done, is a big one. Not everything has been done before. Go and do your work. You can see where it leads and how it fits once it's made.

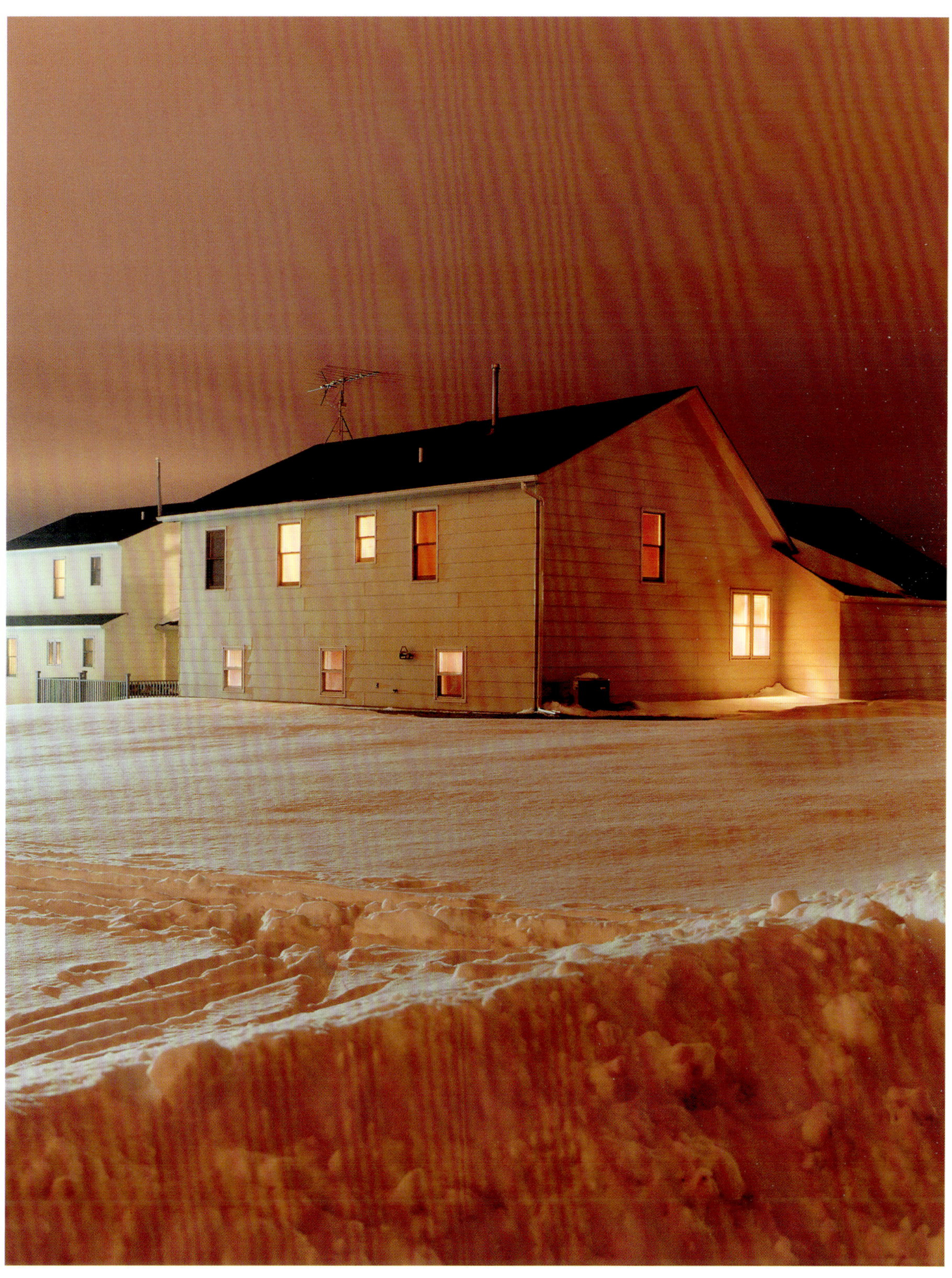

Todd Hido
#2479-a

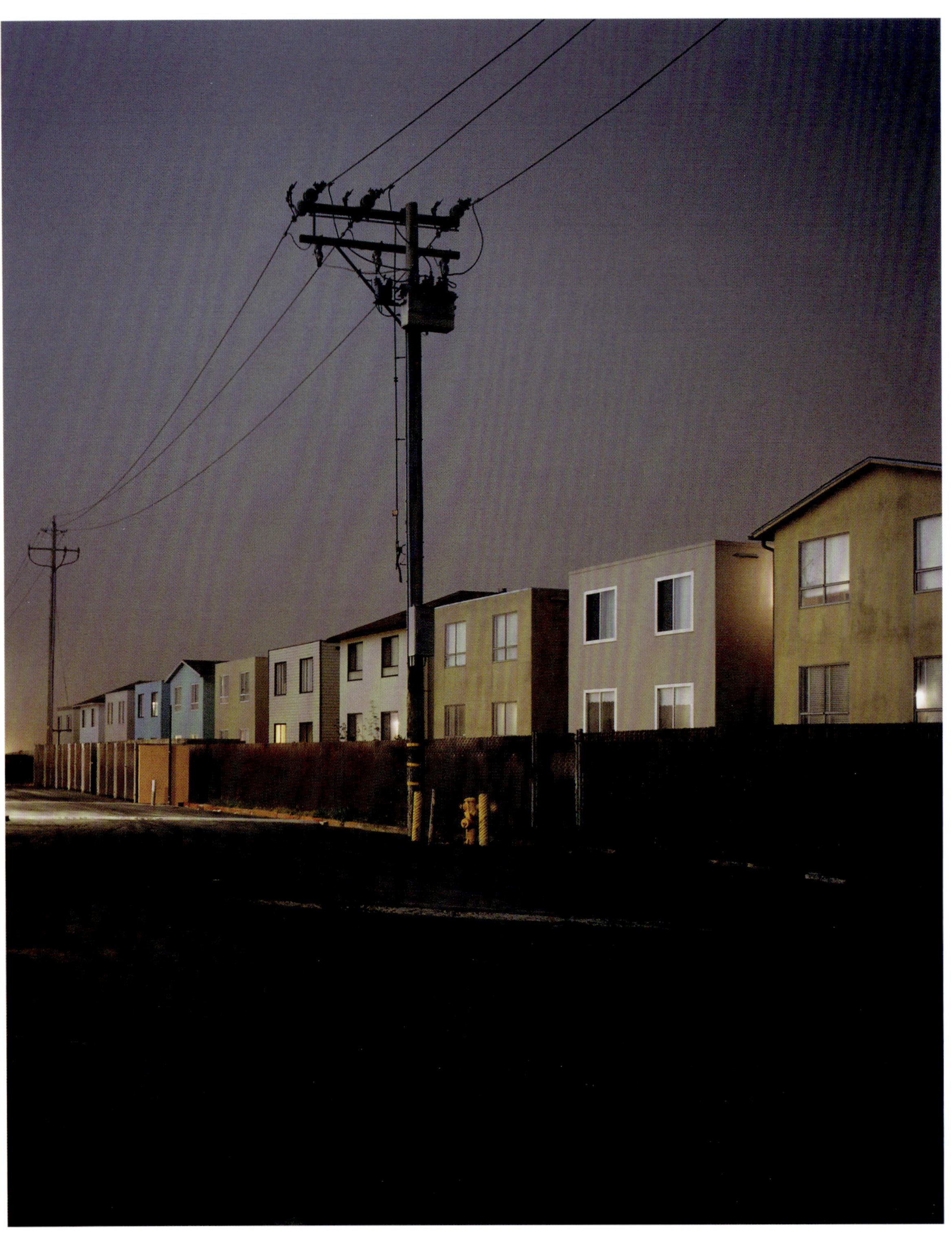

Repetition as Progress

I used to get really freaked out when I didn't have new ideas, thinking, "Oh my God, what am I going to do next?" I thought I had to change everything, and of course, you can't just go and do that because you can't change yourself.

I keep this list of rules for art students in my office, the same list that John Cage kept in his studio. They're by Sister Corita Kent, and the first rule is, "Find a place you trust and then try trusting it for a while." It's okay to stay in the same place for a while and to trust the desire to do so. I'd go to the same suburbs and make pictures of houses at night with lights on. I'd see that a picture was really good and then make another one to see what happened. I'd go back again and again, making pictures in the same places. Slowly but surely the work evolved. I don't think our human nature lets us truly repeat ourselves. Repetition is just part of the creative process.

Frederick Sommer used to say a lot that "variation is change." That's the thing about photography that's so curious. There's something essential in doing the same set of actions over and over again. It's a kind of ruminating. There's a comfort and consistency in the repetition, but it's not too comfortable. You're not bored. There is still something sustaining your interest, pulling you along. You have to trust that you will come up with something different, arrive somewhere new in the process. It may start with making a picture of a house that's orange instead of blue.

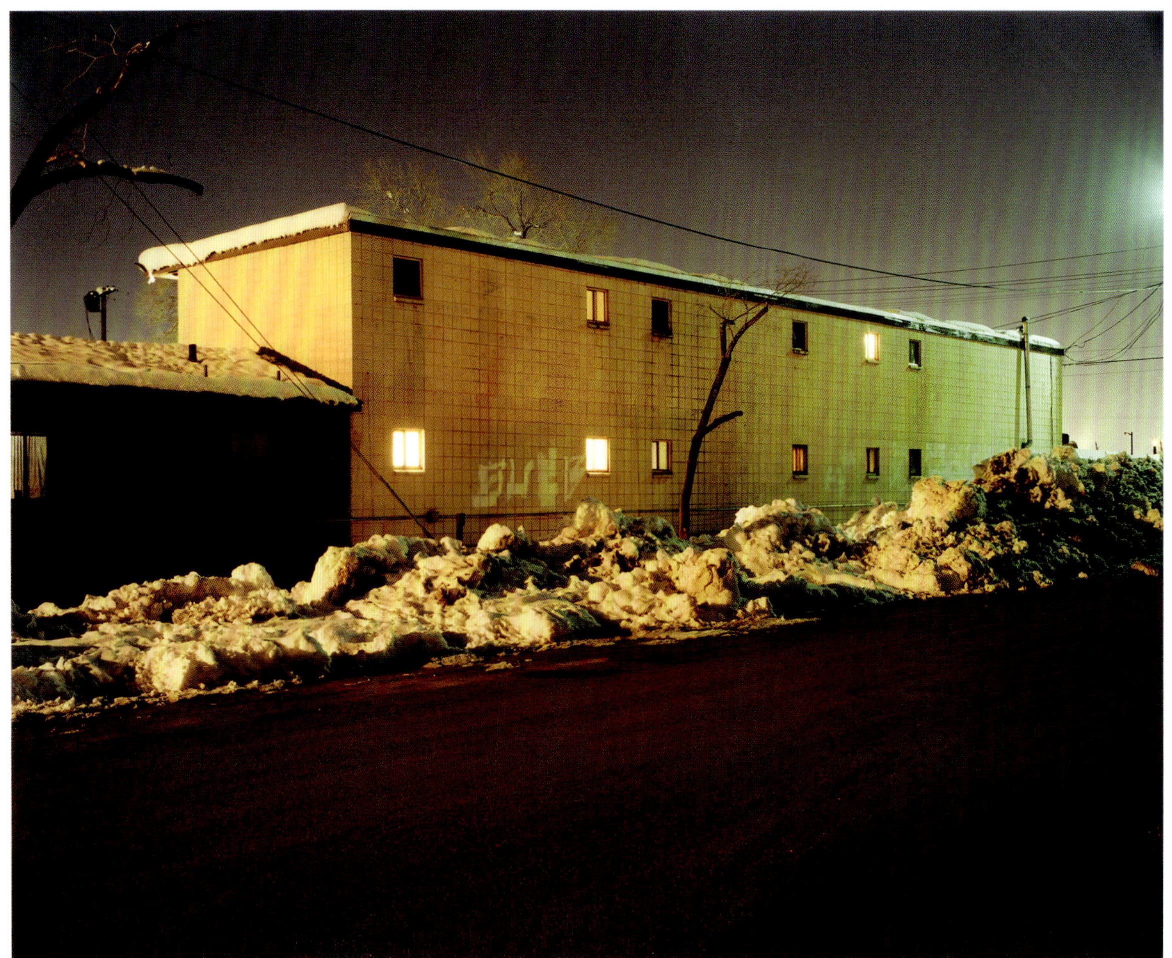

Repetition is your friend and also your enemy. While you want your work to be consistent, to have a style, you've got to strike the right balance between consistency and monotony once you've been working on a project for a while. I remember when I was heavily into photographing the houses at night, there came a point when I was really conscious that the pictures could not all be taken on foggy nights; I couldn't rely on the fog to be the seductive part. I already had a number of those shots and needed to introduce more variation. I had to go out on clear nights also. I needed to go out to the outskirts of the suburbs and take pictures. When I'd hit a critical mass of pictures of houses, I would go out and shoot apartments. I wasn't making huge changes. This type of attentiveness to repetition and variation brings about change.

Todd Hido
#4119

The Power of Beauty

I didn't want to be known as "the guy who does the houses at night." So I decided to change it up. I had made a few landscape pictures while I was out shooting houses. I started to go more in that direction.

My night pictures always had a hard edge to them. But it's very difficult to make a landscape with that kind of edge so the work changed. For the most part, I was not thinking about making a transition from one type of image to another. I just made pictures and they turned out to be more classically beautiful.

With the landscape, I was not afraid of beauty. I allowed myself to approach it, even though this was not popular in the world of photography at the time. I went right up to it and I said, "Hello, beauty." Over time, I started actively invoking the power of beauty, considering the aesthetic potential of the landscape in a new way. Before, I would never have taken a sunset picture. Oh no. That would not have been hard enough.

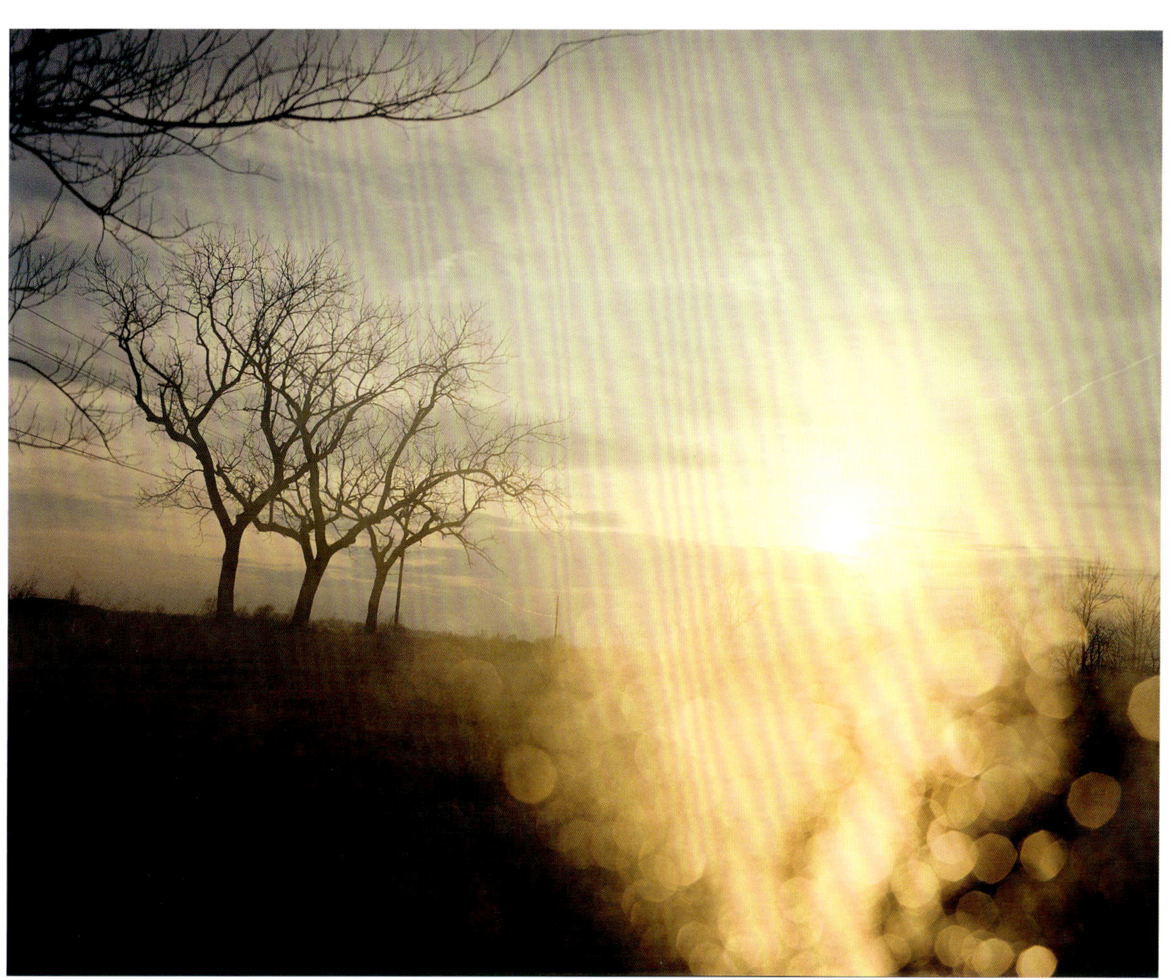

Todd Hido

#3114-b

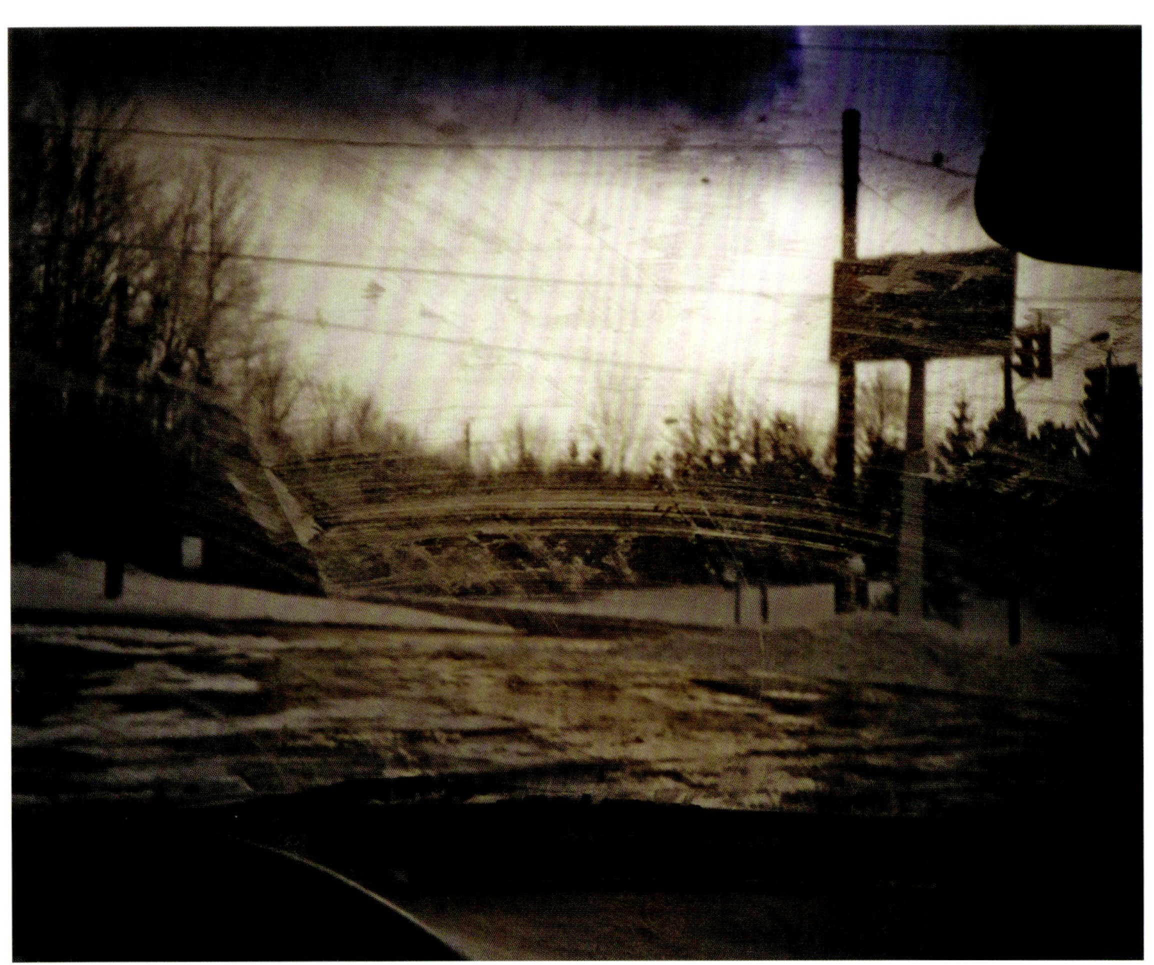

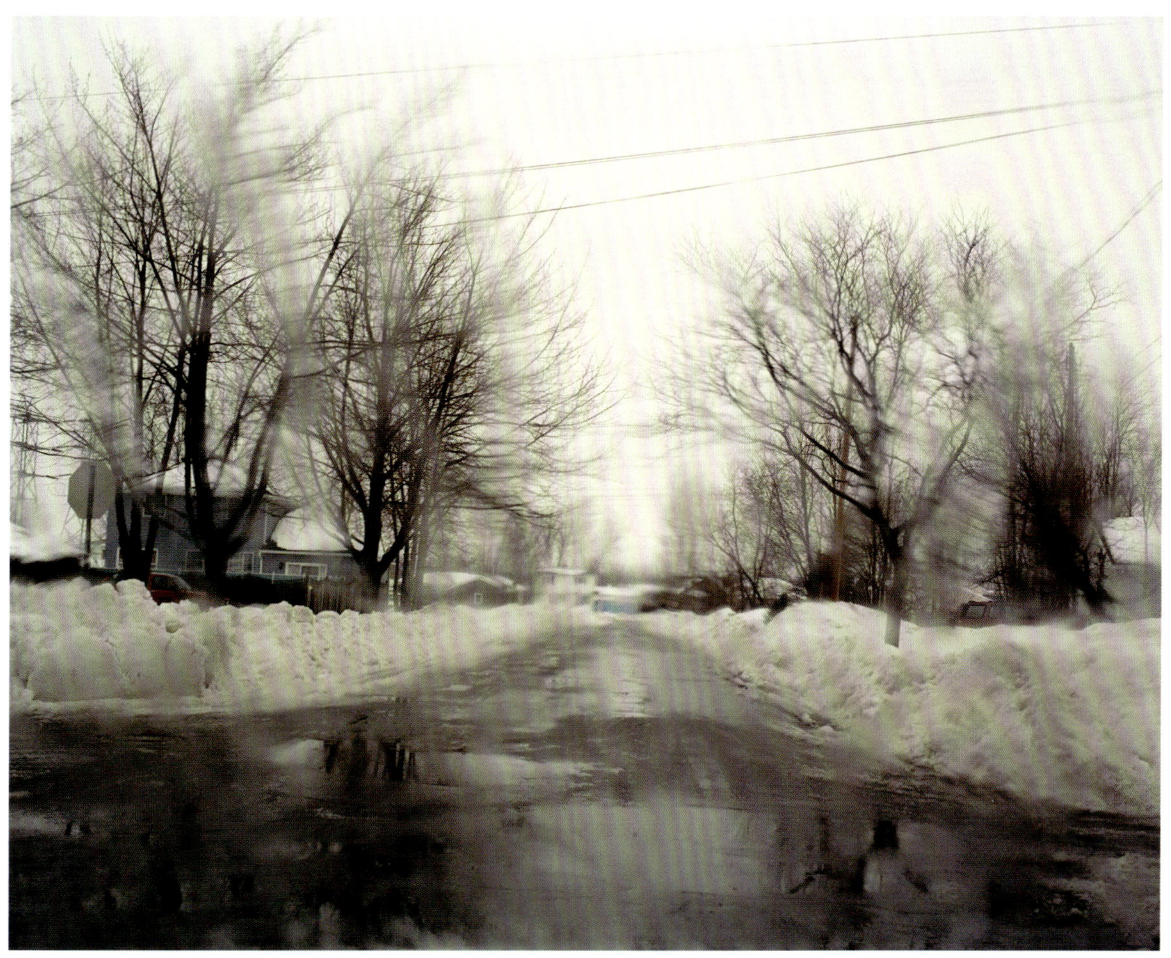

Finding Your Way

I started shooting through the windows of my car by accident. It was raining one day when I was out taking pictures in the suburbs. When I stopped at an intersection, all the water rushed off the roof of the car and poured down the windshield, creating an expressive and painterly scene in front of me. I took the picture. That's how things happen. Sometimes you discover your methods of working by just making photographs. You go out, walk around or drive around, and make some pictures, expose film. And then through the act of making lots of pictures, something clicks. You have to trust in that; you have to trust in shooting blind. You have to trust that even though you feel like you are going through the motions and there's no real destination, you are finding your way creatively.

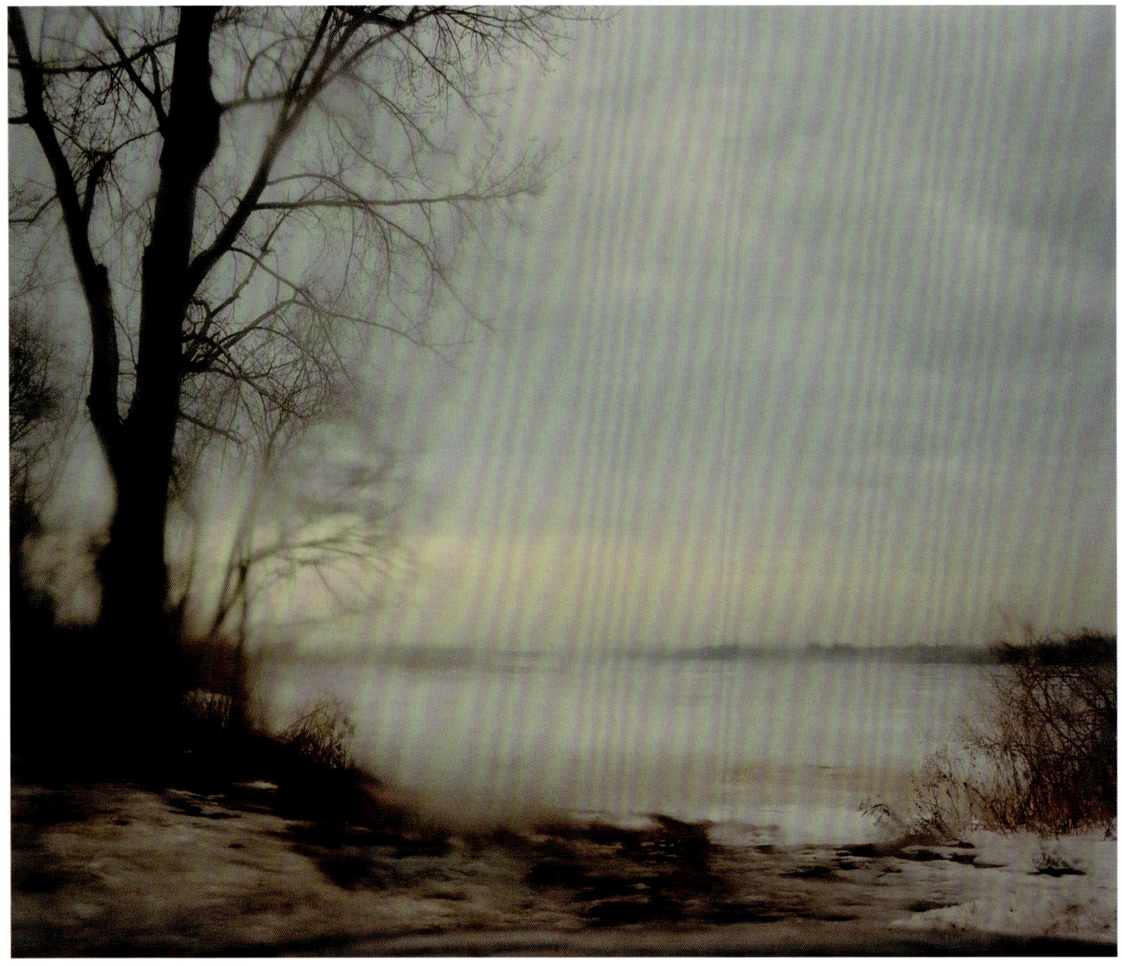

You can't look at what's popular at the moment and then simply go and repeat it. That's a recipe for disaster.

You'll make empty art if you try that approach or only care about success. You'll always be chasing something, because trends change constantly. One minute, cold, crisp, and conceptual German photography is the bee's knees, and then the next minute, emotional documentary work is hot.

When I started in my career it was very much the era of theory and post-modernism. Subjective emotion and beauty were not on the radar. It was cliché to have anything to do with that. I was encouraged to shoot from a uniform distance, to use a more neutral color palette, to work more conceptually, to take a more objective stance—basically to work like I had studied with the Bechers in Düsseldorf.

But that advice, well meaning as it was, didn't sit right with me. Those weren't the kinds of pictures that I wanted to make, and I knew better than to follow that path. There are always going to be way too many people giving you

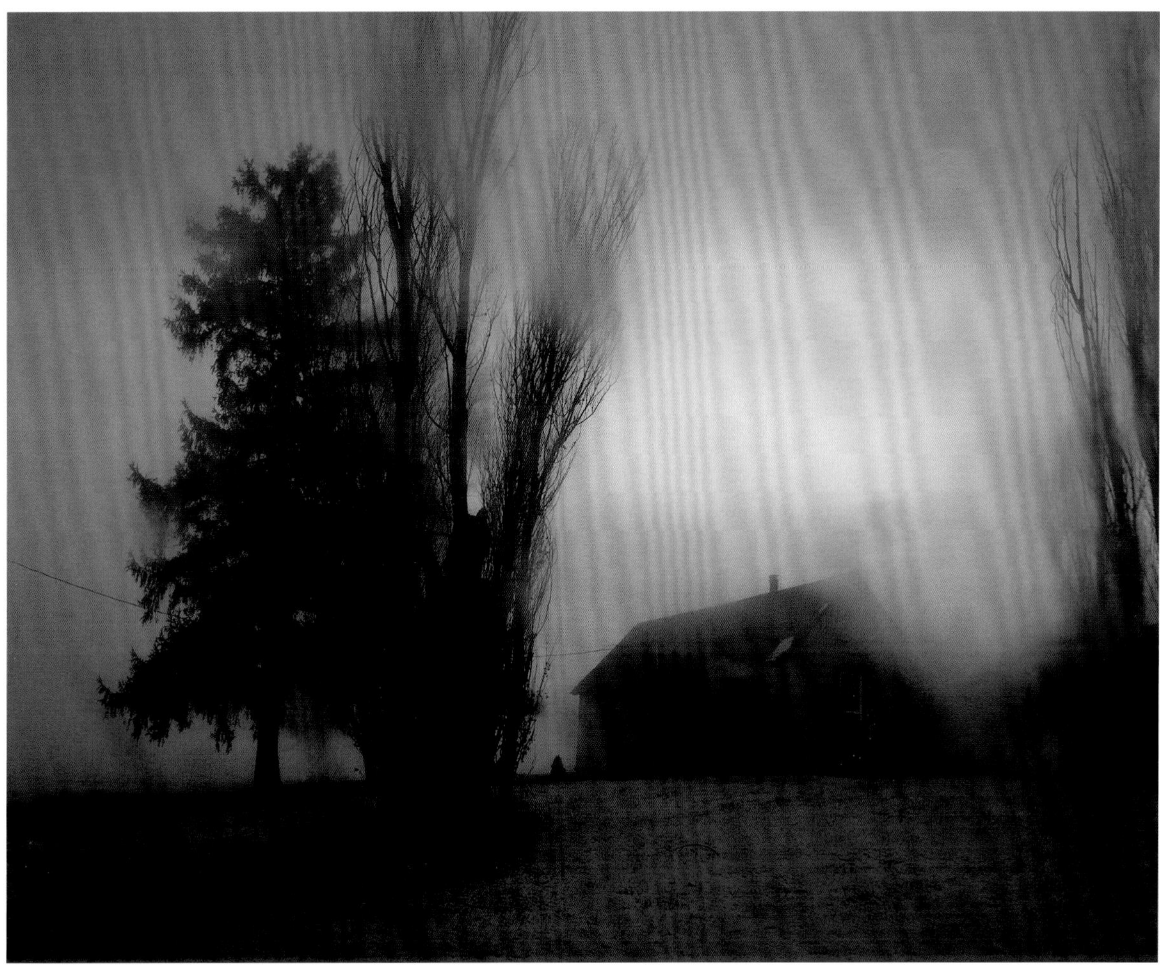

their opinion. When you do get advice, it's important that you, as an artist, know what to leave and what to take on and consider. You can't become somebody you're not.

It has served me well throughout my career to follow my own instincts. I learned early on that I should just do what I wanted to do, and I wanted to keep my work emotional and subjective. Really, I couldn't do anything other than that. I can honestly say that even if I had not achieved any level of success with my work, I would still make it because I need and want to make it.

Left
Todd Hido
#10253

Above
Todd Hido
#9202

In and Out of Focus

I love driving around in the rain. There's nothing else like it. I love the sound of the rain on the car. I like how the world becomes distorted through wet windows. For the most part, I shoot my landscapes from the car.

There are a number of sophisticated things operating in the landscapes. Things are in and out of focus. You come to crossroads. You can see some trees while others are obscured by rain. I consciously make those decisions. When a raindrop is going down the windshield, I'm like, "Oh!" and stop the car. I'm moving my camera while I shoot to get the points of focus in the right place. I think of it like I would a still life. It's the bits of minutiae that make up the larger picture. You have to pay close attention and carefully place all that stuff in the frame so that the picture works.

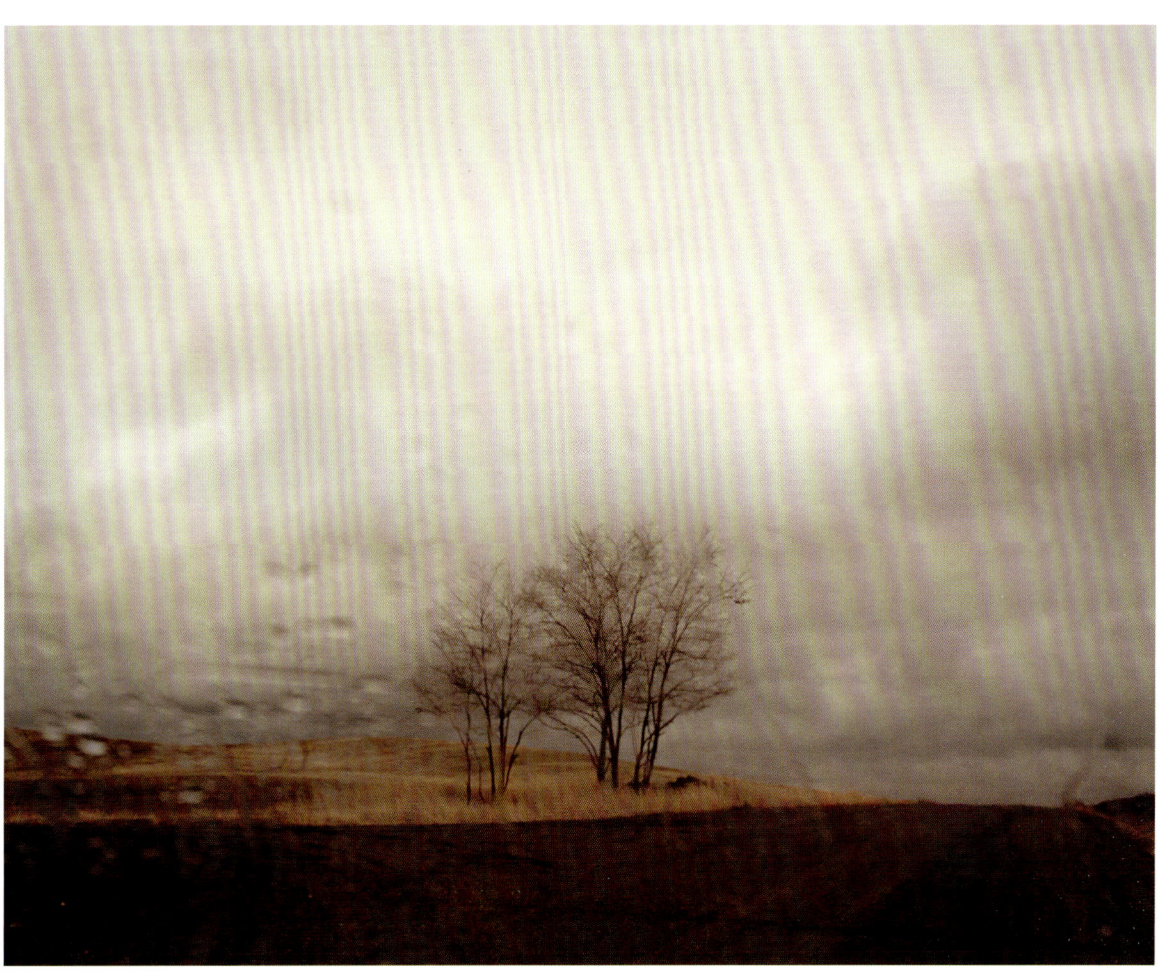

Todd Hido
#3225

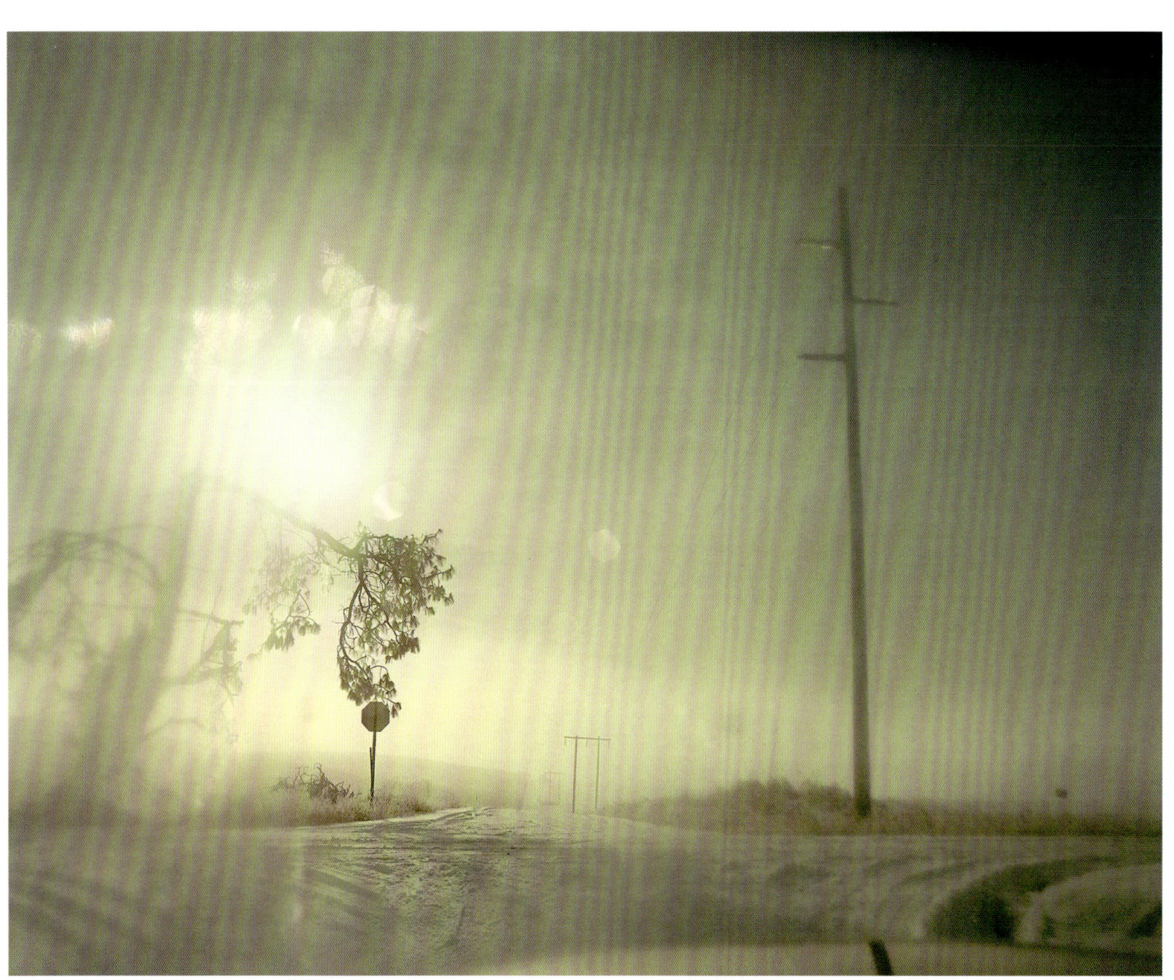

Todd Hido
#6097

This picture is kind of confusing, which is why it's interesting. It was a very foggy day, and was the moment when the fog began to lift. There was water on the window of the car, and the sun was shining right into the camera. The diffused light is doing the work here: I'm often shooting straight into the light so shooting through a foggy, dirty, or wet windshield helps cut the brightness and make for a more painterly image. I happened to be at a four-way rural intersection, and there was a tree drooping down. This is just one of those moments that was meant to be. I didn't have a plan—it happened, and I recognized when to press the shutter.

In their own weird way, the landscapes tell the viewer how to feel. Feel cold. Feel isolated. Feel lost. The road appears in most of my pictures, so you know you're on a path. Sometimes the road stretches deep into the distance, toward an unknown destination, or infinity. At other times, the pictures place you at a crossroads, where you have to choose which way to turn, or at the end.

Sometimes you take a picture but only figure out later why it works: What are the elements that made it a success that created this feeling? And how can I do it again? Or what does it all add up to? I've come to see that pictures that are both in focus and out of focus from the car are like memories—certain parts are really clear and other parts are hazy. That's the thing that resonates for me in the landscape pictures; they reflect how the mind works. They're a metaphor for memory.

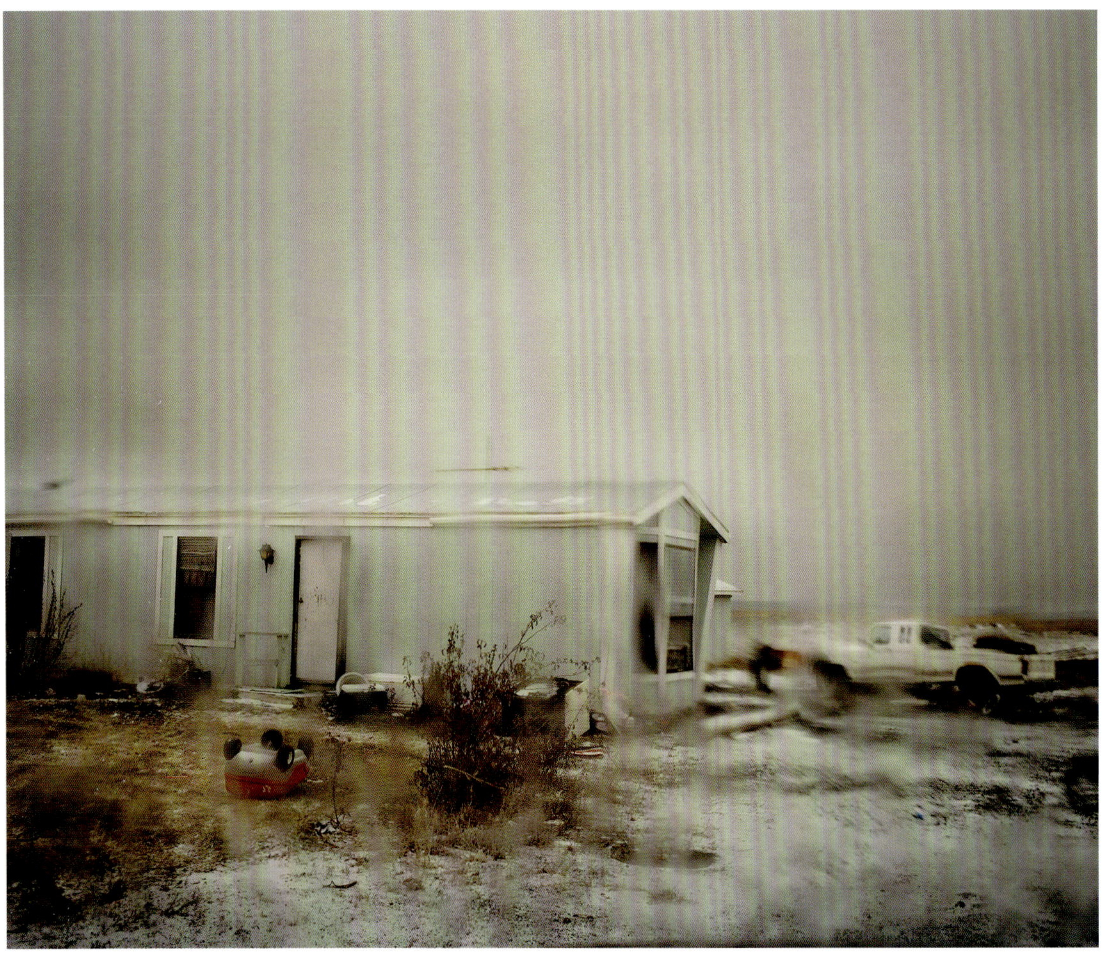

An Intimate Distance

Shooting through the windshield intensifies the pictures; it heightens the sense of memory and also grounds the picture squarely in the physical world. It's one thing to take a picture of a snowy landscape. It's another level of difficulty to take that picture in a way that actually conveys the feeling of cold and damp.

And that has to do with looking through the water on the windshield. The camera is right at the windshield, and I'm shooting through that water. I'm inside, but somehow the picture has the feeling of the outside world.

Robert Frank's picture *View from Hotel Window—Butte, Montana* (1956), which he shot through a hotel room window has been a big influence. There's something about those curtains he is shooting through; it's almost as if you have to push them aside to see the melancholy town better. They add an intimate feeling to the picture because as a viewer, you're standing in Frank's shoes looking out that window. You are aware of him as the photographer. And I think that's precisely what's happening when I shoot through the window of the car.

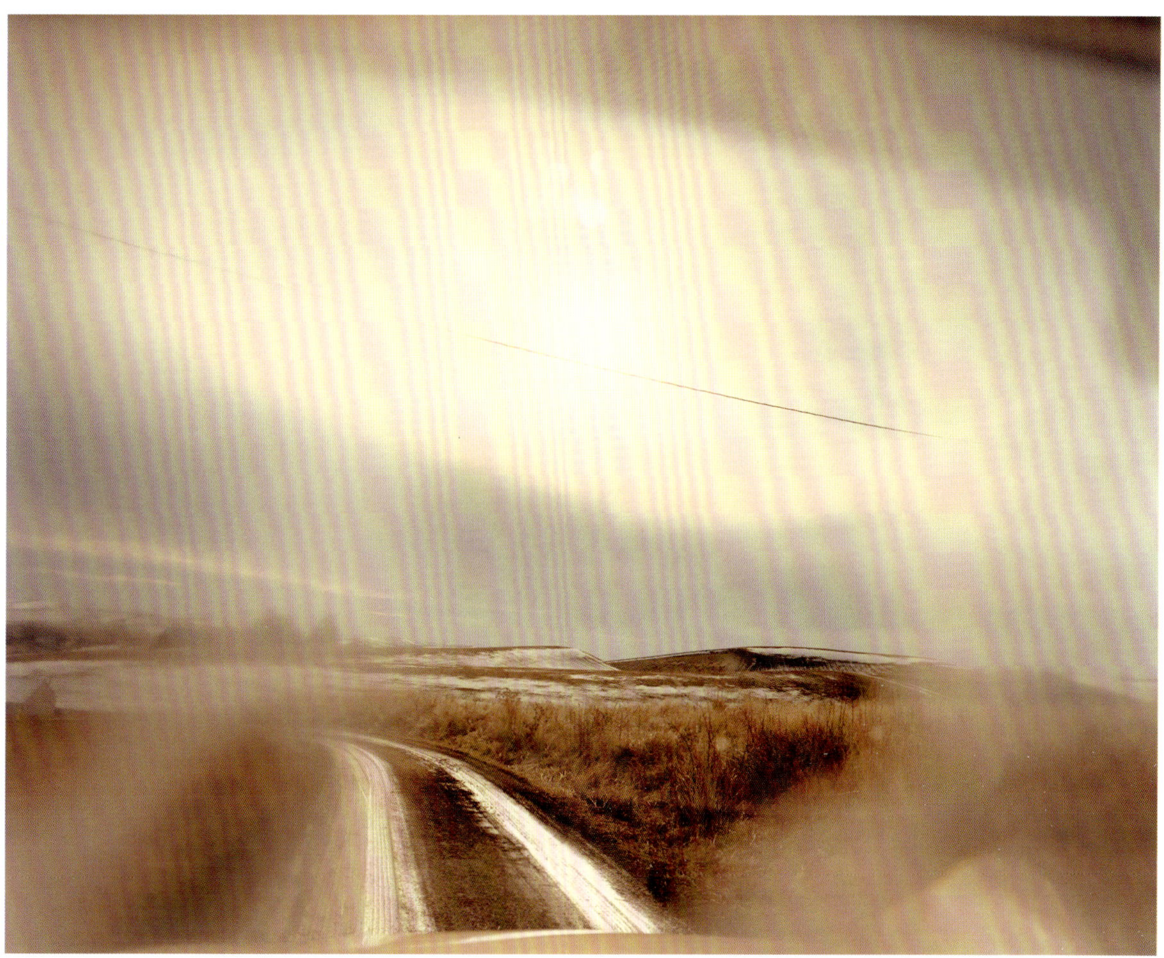

The viewer is situated close to what's outside, and at the same time, my presence as the photographer inside the car becomes part of the picture. That's my breath fogging up the windows. A landscape could depict vastness or distance, but these elements keep the outside close—personal and intimate.

Left
Todd Hido
#9197

Above
Todd Hido
#6237

The Color of Emotion

Another primary thing that conveys feeling in photographs is color. Blue will almost always read as cold to us, especially in a landscape. Green represents growth or sickness, depending on the hue. Colors bring their own meanings and moods to a picture.

When I first started photographing, I was shooting black-and-white. I'd never really shot in color because I didn't have access to a color darkroom and whenever I had worked in color, I sent the negatives to a lab, and they would always create a neutral print. I wasn't interested in that; I found the print to be too real. There was something about it that too closely referenced the real world instead of this imaginary world that I was trying to create.

At grad school, I would see people printing color in the darkroom, and so I started experimenting with it too. When I started printing color in the darkroom myself, I remembered learning how to make an interpretive print in black and white with Roy DeCarava years before. I had signed up to take a workshop at Anderson Ranch, and it was supposed to be taught by Sam Abell, the great *National Geographic* photographer from Ohio, but he canceled. Roy DeCarava taught the workshop instead, and it ended up being a black-and-white darkroom class. I would bring my print out of the darkroom in the wet tray and show it to Roy. Each time he said, "Make it darker. Make it darker." I saw that though pictures turn out a certain way in their raw negative form, you can push them in a whole different direction in the printing. That's largely what I've done in the darkroom for years. My pictures don't materialize into form straight from the camera; I choose the way they look and feel afterward. Taking the picture is just the starting point. Often my contact sheets look nothing like the final print. I'm very manipulative in the darkroom, and now, on the computer.

That one-week workshop completely influenced my whole career—learning that a print can be interpreted to look any way you want it to look. There is no right way. It's totally subjective.

When I started experimenting with printing in color, I thought about what it would be like if Roy DeCarava was standing outside the darkroom giving me advice. He might say, "Make the color totally gone." Or, "Make the color super blue."

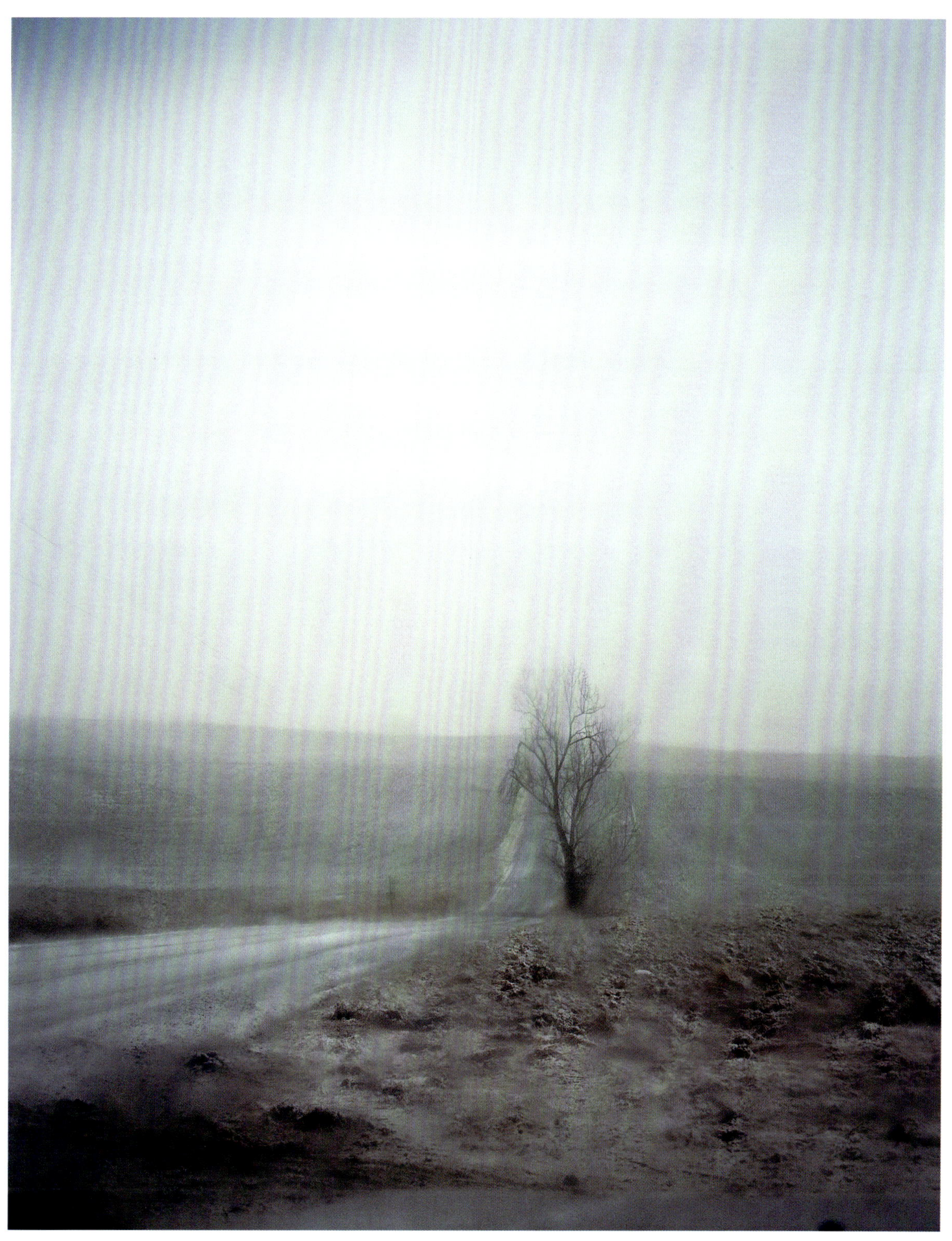

Todd Hido
#5157

Todd Hido
#10320

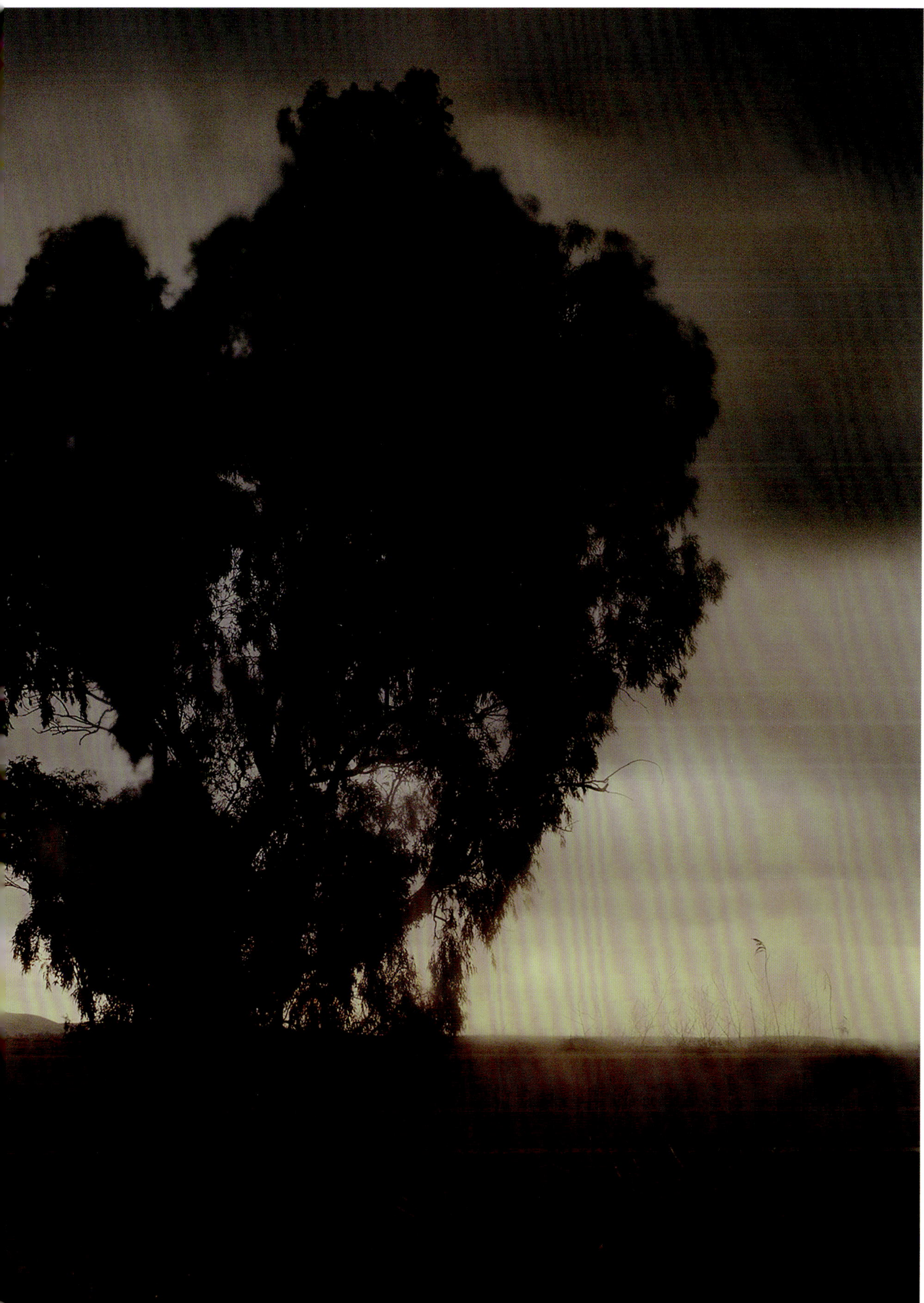

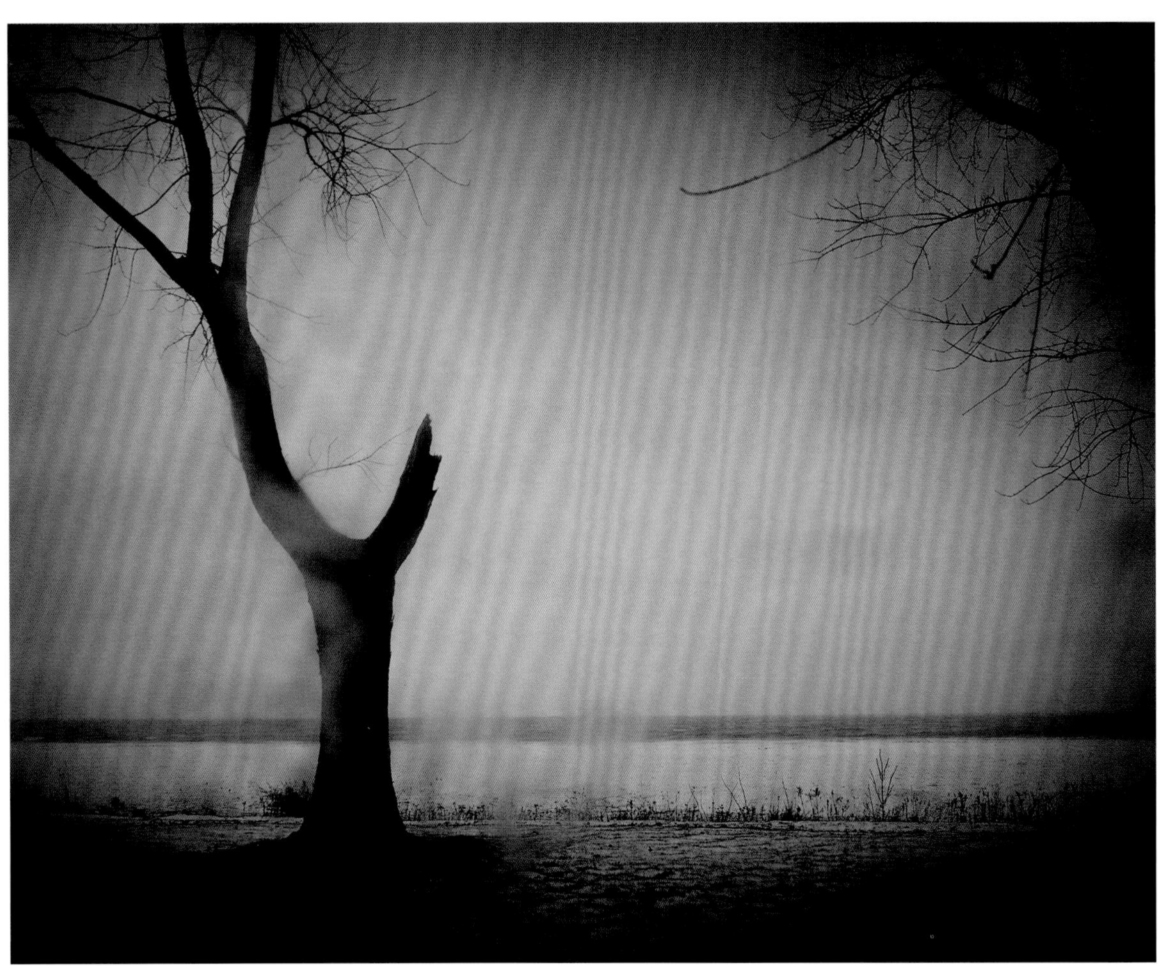

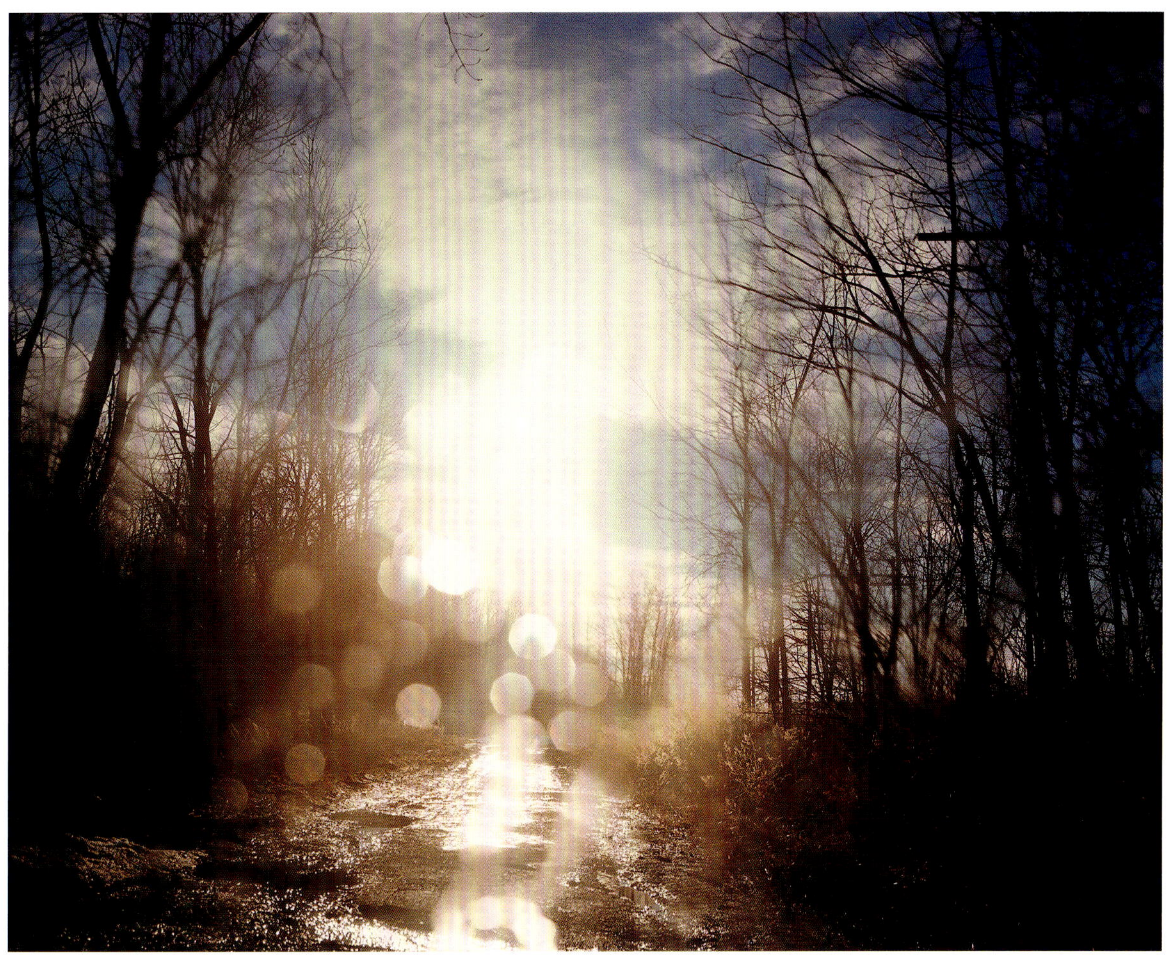

I photograph like a documentarian, but I print like a painter.

I don't like to set things up when I'm shooting. I really prefer to photograph what I find. The interpretation comes in making the print.

I was never really instructed in how to print in color, so I adjusted the colors in my photographs to be whatever I felt they should look like or convey. The way I use color is very subjective. The picture on the left is a super-cold gray. A neutral print of this would be unimpressive. But the color here reflects the feeling of the place: middle of the winter, edge of the lake, wind blowing, ice-cold.

Then when the sun comes out, the photograph has an entirely different feeling to it. But these colors don't reflect what it actually looked like. I like colors that are more muted and softer than in reality. I'm not married to reality; I don't feel I have to faithfully describe a place. I add my own emotional content in the choices I make in the printing process. Color absolutely sets a mood. There's no question about it. When I'm choosing the colors, anything goes, but I still want the picture to feel like it could be real, like it could have happened.

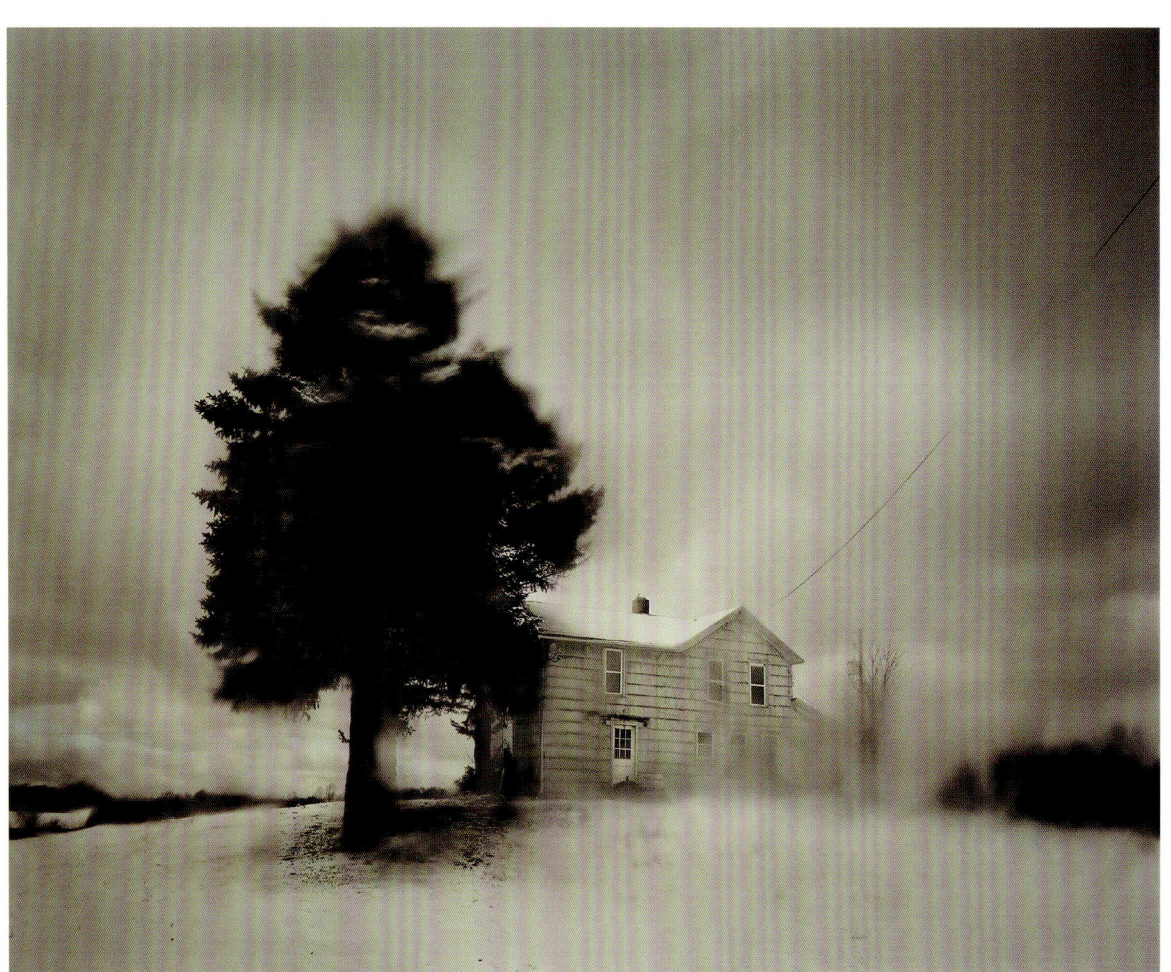

Many Small Decisions

For years, I used a tripod. I would never take a picture without one. That was when I was shooting interiors and houses at night.

When I was starting to do the landscape pictures through the car window, I started holding the camera. I had to hold it because you can't really set up a tripod in the car. Actually, one time I did put a tripod in the car. I figured out how to make the legs sit in the few places they could, but it was near impossible. If I had had to drive the car, it would've been a joke.

Ultimately, I started holding my Pentax camera and shooting the houses and landscapes from the car. The photos were all crooked. So then I thought, "Well, what happens when you tilt the camera more purposefully?" Psychologically, when you tilt the camera, everything is a little off. It has a Hitchcock-like effect. There's a specific thing about tilting the frame we recognize from movies; it can signify that something bad is about to happen. And I like to use that.

What's interesting is how that idea came from a simple decision. I've made some really wonderful pictures that way—as a result of this "tripod or no tripod" business. Notice how the house here is not straight. If I'd used a tripod, it would have been. The simple decisions and questions matter. They change photographs drastically and they can completely change the way you work.

Making decisions is one of the most critical things in art making. You're always in a state of deciding. What camera am I going use? Am I going to shoot this in black and white or color? Horizontal or vertical? Am I going to print this in Inkjet or LightJet? Larry Sultan used to say that the act of making art is the act of making many, many, many small decisions. Each question you encounter can lead you down a particular path. If you can be decisive and move forward through the decisions step by step, you'll be more successful. The real question is: What's right for you right now? And realizing that what's right for you changes over time.

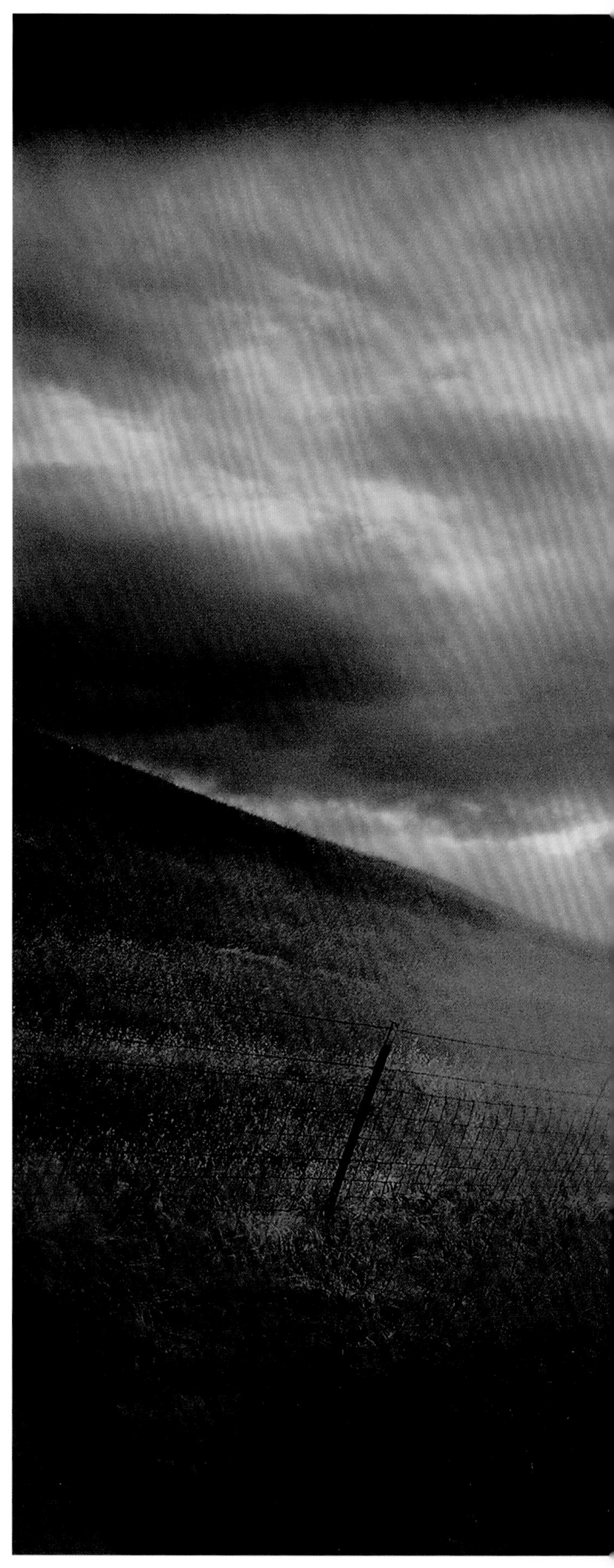

Todd Hido
#3277

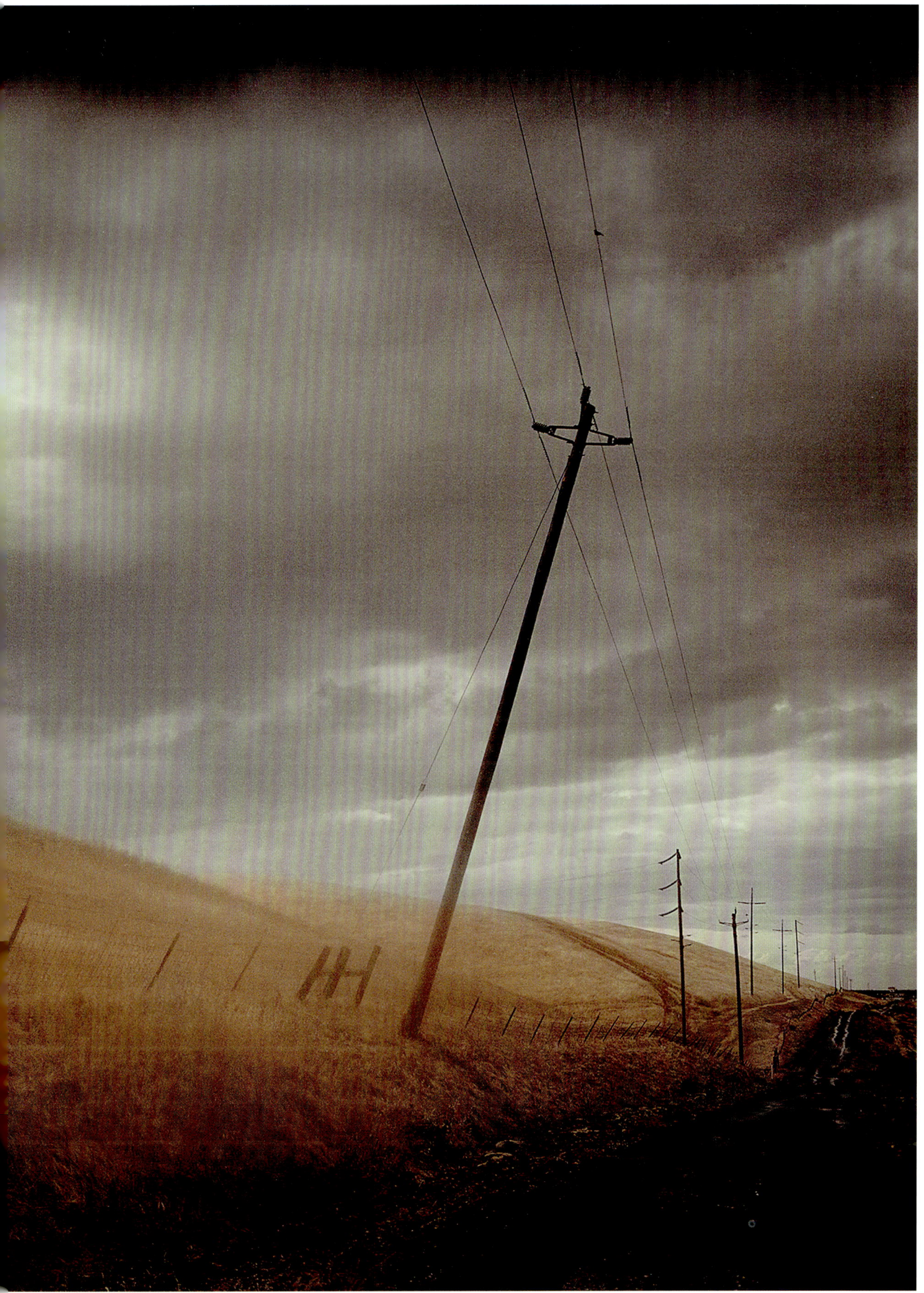

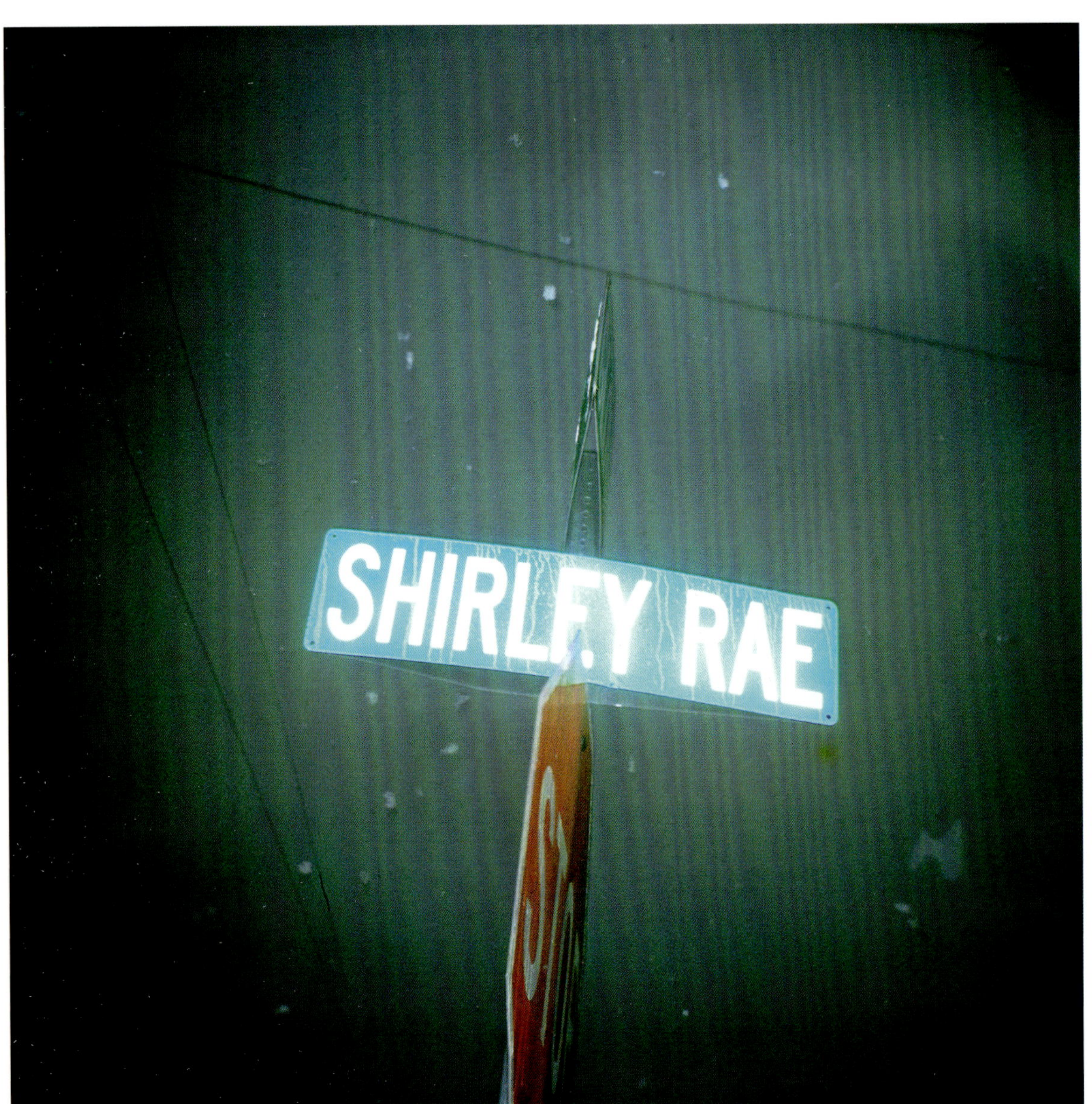
SHIRLEY RAE

Concepts and Contradictions

There are no rules. But sometimes you need parameters. They could be conceptual. Sometimes, there's value in just naming what you're doing at the moment as a concept: "I photograph houses at night." You can then add to the concept, like, "I also create a mood. I look for moody things at night." Or, "I only photograph on cloudy days." The concept can change and evolve. You can always modify it at any point because it's yours.

Your parameters should be flexible enough, though, that you can still just shoot whatever moves you. Photograph whatever catches your eye, whatever gets your ass out of the chair to go photograph. Take the picture and see what happens, because you never know. Sometimes the world looks different in photographs. Like Garry Winogrand said, "I photograph to find out what something will look like photographed." This leaves the door open for surprise. Often with the unexpected, with contradiction, there's growth.

Most of my landscape work I made by just going out and taking pictures. I wasn't shooting for anything specific. I was not thinking, "I have a book coming up and I need to shoot some landscapes." They were the work I made in order to make work. I would tell myself, "If it's raining, I'm going out to take pictures." The photos came out of those little events, those small decisions.

I also started making shorter trips out of town—to Ohio when I could and also to places closer by that spoke to me. A two-hour plane ride could take me to eastern Washington, for instance. I love working this way because sometimes it's hard for me to focus on my work at home; there's too much going on. I may want to leave the house at 10:00, but I end up leaving at 12:30 because I answer the phone and get pulled into other things. I'm a single father of twins. It's not always possible to be creative whenever I want. That's not real life. If I can get away for a short trip, I am not only transported to a different location but a different mental space; and I know my time there will be dedicated to taking pictures.

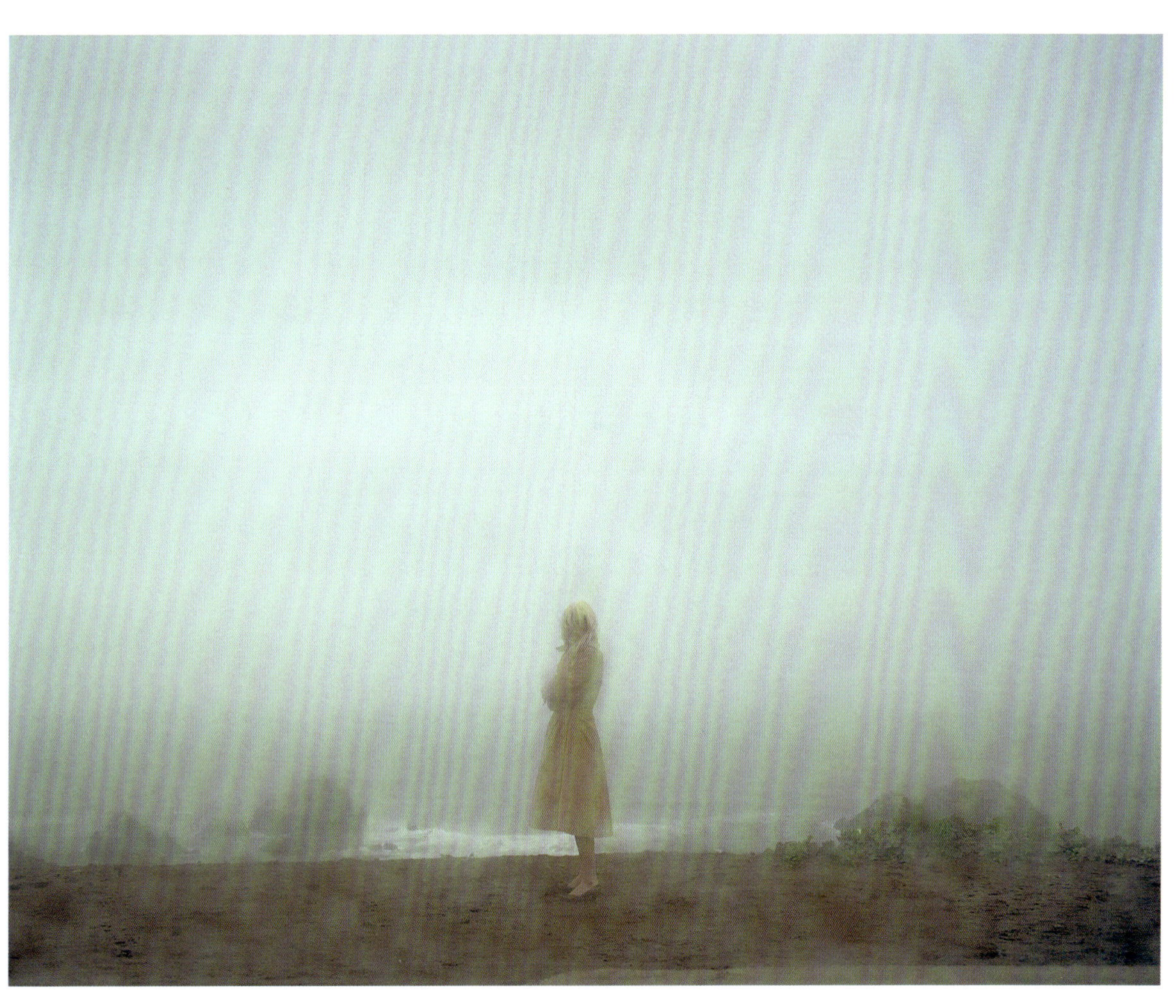

Knowing When

How do you know when you're done with a project? I kept on making the landscape pictures because I was still captivated by the subject. I wasn't making them for art's sake; I was making them because I needed to make them.

And so I'd say you're done with something when you stop getting out of your car to photograph it, or when you stop getting your camera out of your bag to take a picture. That's when you're done: when you're not compelled to shoot the subject anymore.

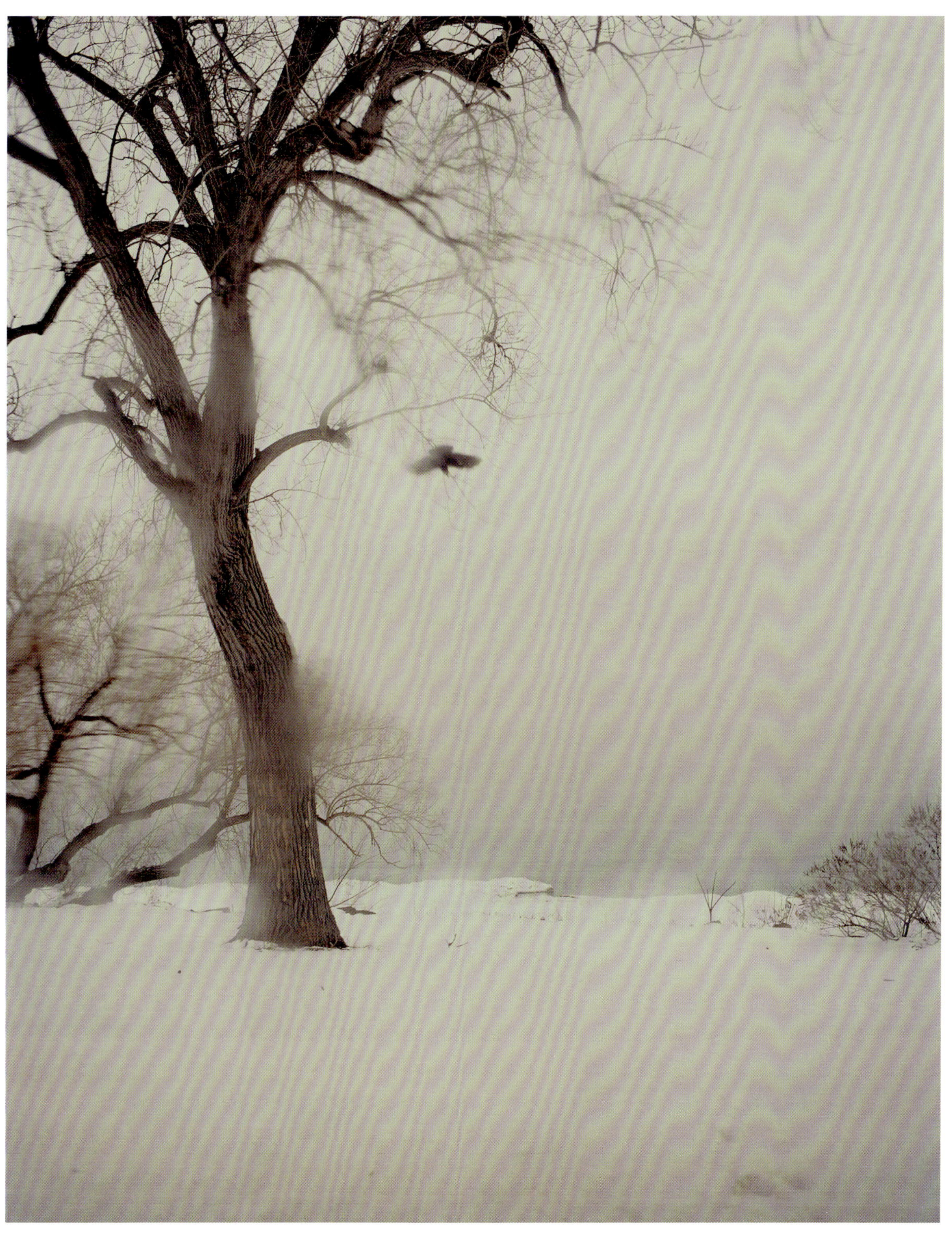

Todd Hido
#10192

63

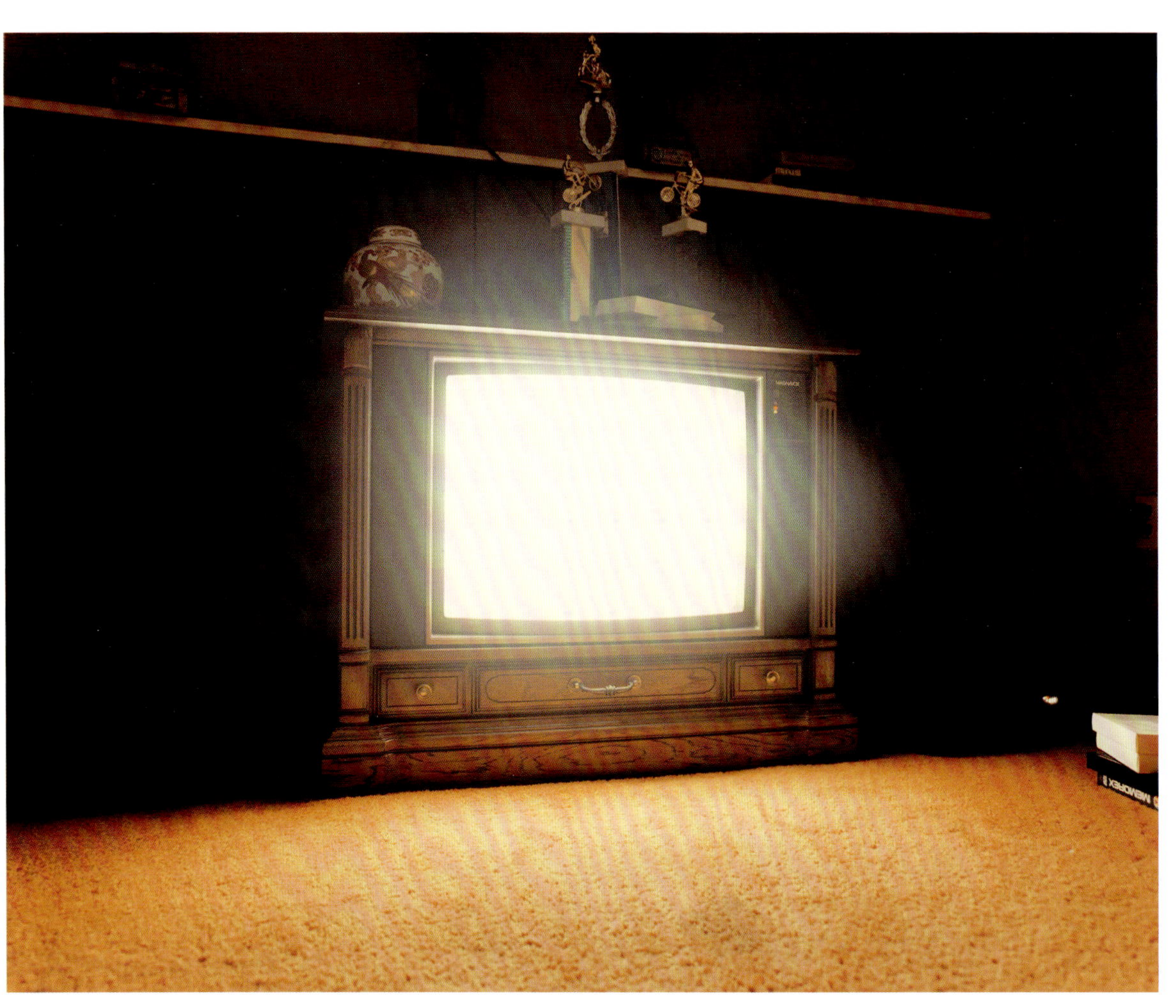

Interior Spaces

As I was shooting exteriors, I was standing on the outside looking in. The next natural step was to go inside. Clearly, I was not going to get invited into the homes I was photographing in the landscapes, so I started shooting interiors when I went home to Ohio. When you grow up and move away, your old childhood bedroom becomes foreign again. It's locked in the past where you used to live. I was blind to home when I lived there, but when I visit from California, I am very aware of the interior of the house. My antenna is picking up signals of the past.

      I consider this photograph a mini-tribute to Hiroshi Sugimoto, with his long exposures in theaters where there's no image on the screen. This is the television in my parents' house, the TV that corrupted me. Those are my BMX trophies on the top. The wood console television and the wood paneling and shag carpet activate a sense of the past. This is not now.

      I wanted to convey a kind of charge to the space so I shot it from a watching distance to the TV and from the ground. I wanted to capture the feeling of sitting in front of that television on that shag carpet in my half-finished basement family room and watching endless hours of television. The blank screen conveys a kind of emptiness, and the light from the TV on the carpet emphasizes the perspective, which makes the picture personal. You get the sense that this is the room where I would sit with a bag of Doritos and a two-liter of Mountain Dew watching TV after school and late into the night.

Surface Memories

Anyone who's ever renovated a house knows that interiors are all about surfaces. The kind of flooring, the kind of wallpaper, the color of the paint—these all add up to create the environment of a house. I think the surfaces that we grew up with are imprinted in our memory in a really deep way. People respond immediately to 1970s wood paneling, for example. They recognize that it's not a typical part of our surroundings anymore. So this one detail can carry you back to the past and elicit memories. I think there's something profound about how that happens. A picture is not contained by its frame.

The space we exist in within the home is incredibly important. Each room in the house has a different meaning. A picture taken from the perspective of someone watching TV in the basement has a different meaning than one of a bedroom because so many different activities happen in that room. Certain things happen in a bed, and a photograph of a single bed tells a different story than one of a double bed. All of these details matter to the mood and meaning of a picture. A picture of a bed is not necessarily a picture of a bed—it could be a picture about a relationship, it could be a picture about sexuality. It could be a picture about loss or love, or it could be a loveless picture.

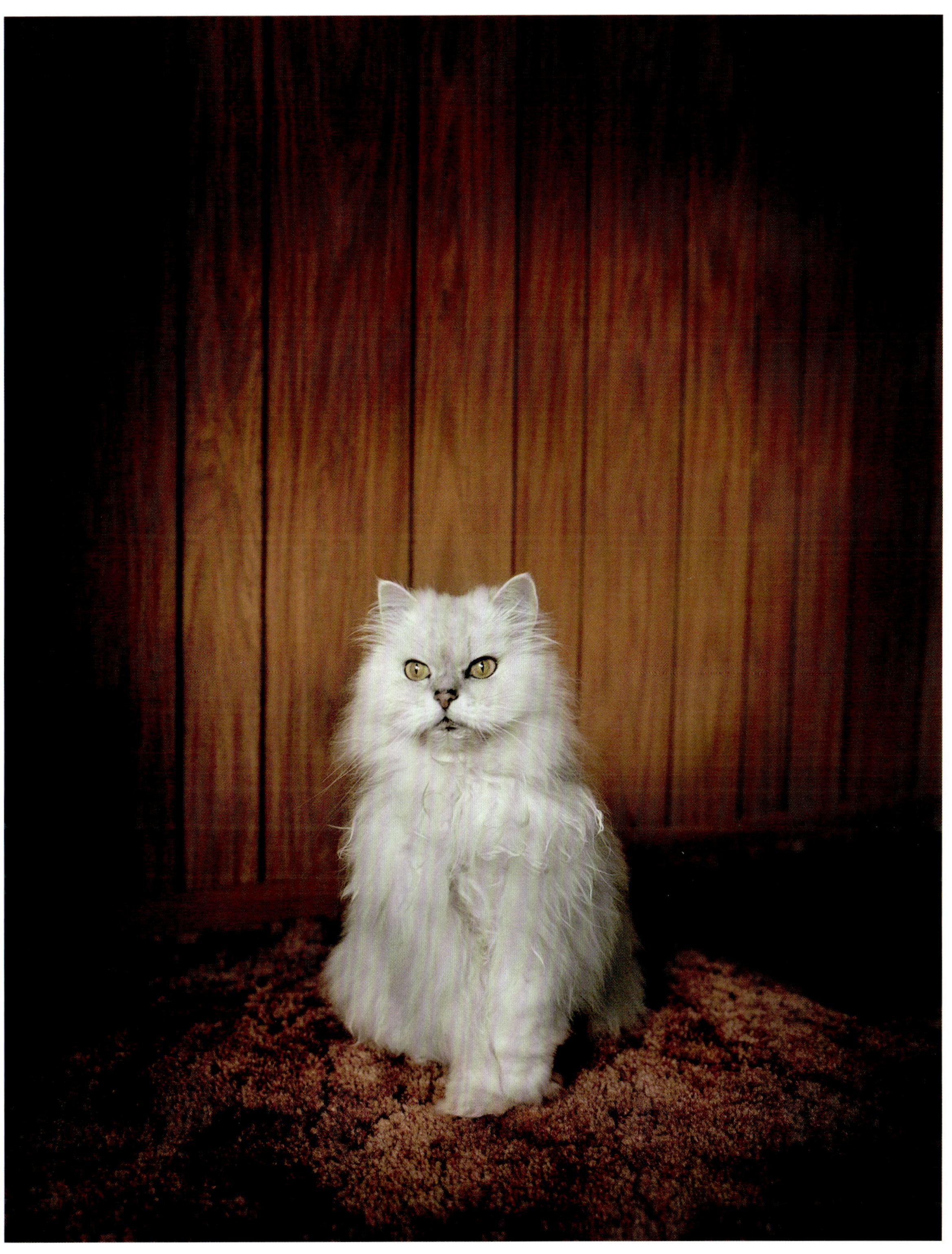

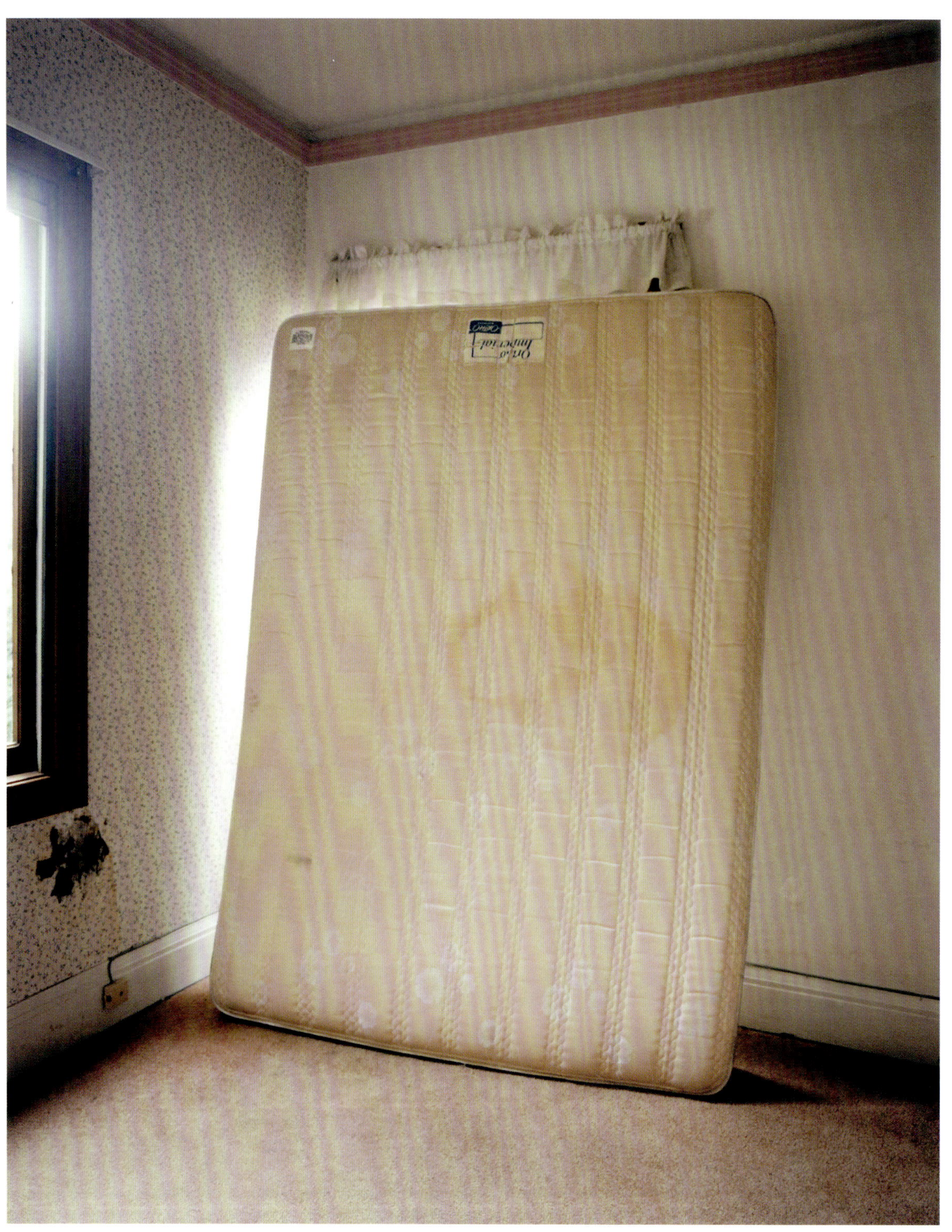

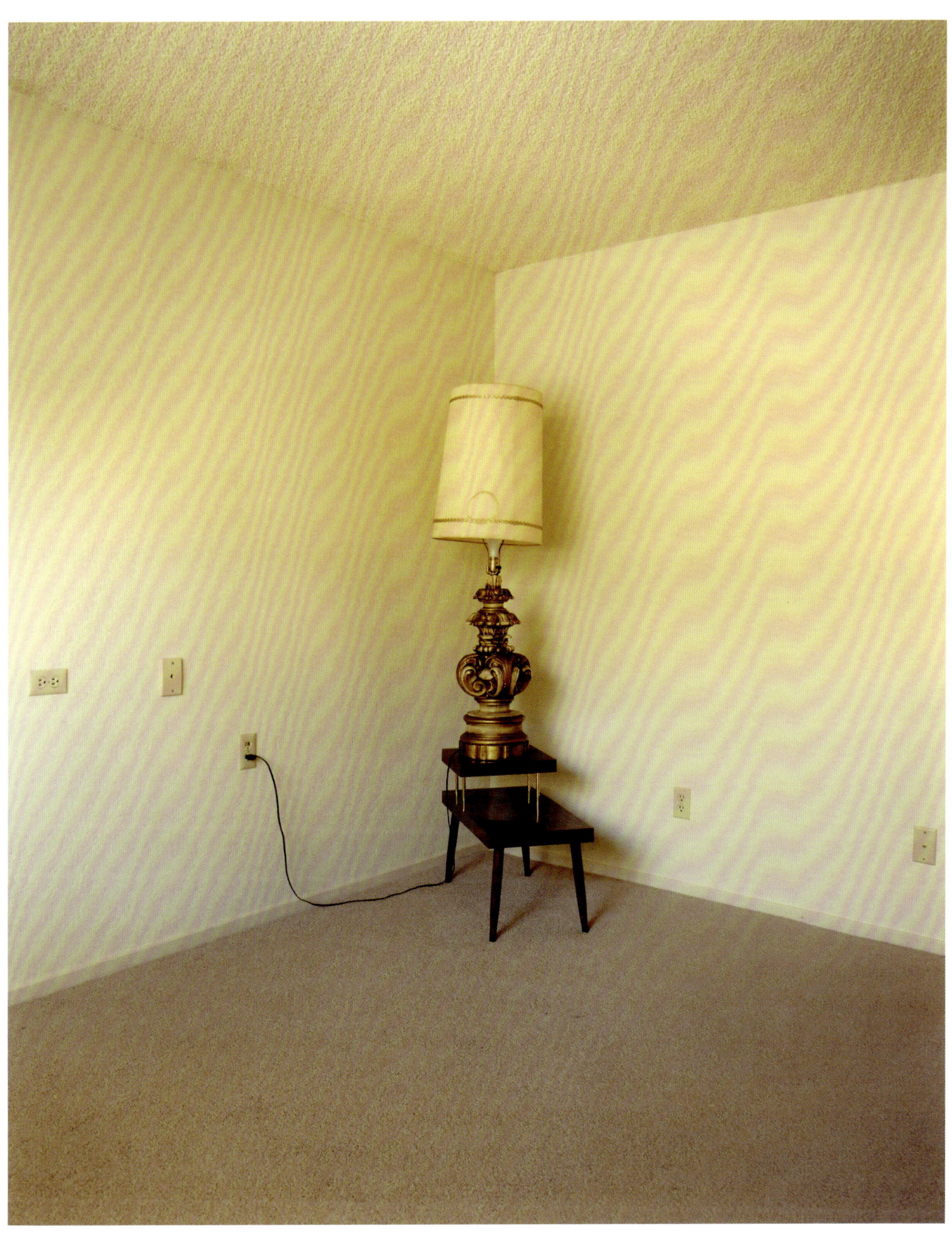

I went home for Christmas and made this photograph of my bed. I was paying attention to little moments like this that revealed something about my family. This was my bed as a boy, and now I was sleeping in that bed as an adult. The day before, I had been in sunny California, but I woke up in Ohio, and turning around, saw the dreary winter light of my boyhood. I had my mom go get my camera because I didn't want to move from the spot.

That pillow caught my attention. It was stripped bare, and I was struck by the kind of bare-bones life it revealed. My family knew I was coming to visit from California. Did anybody bother to put a pillowcase on my pillow? No.

A viewer doesn't know these details or exactly how I feel about the scene, but there's something heightened in the tactility of the picture that intimates there's meaning there, a story to be told.

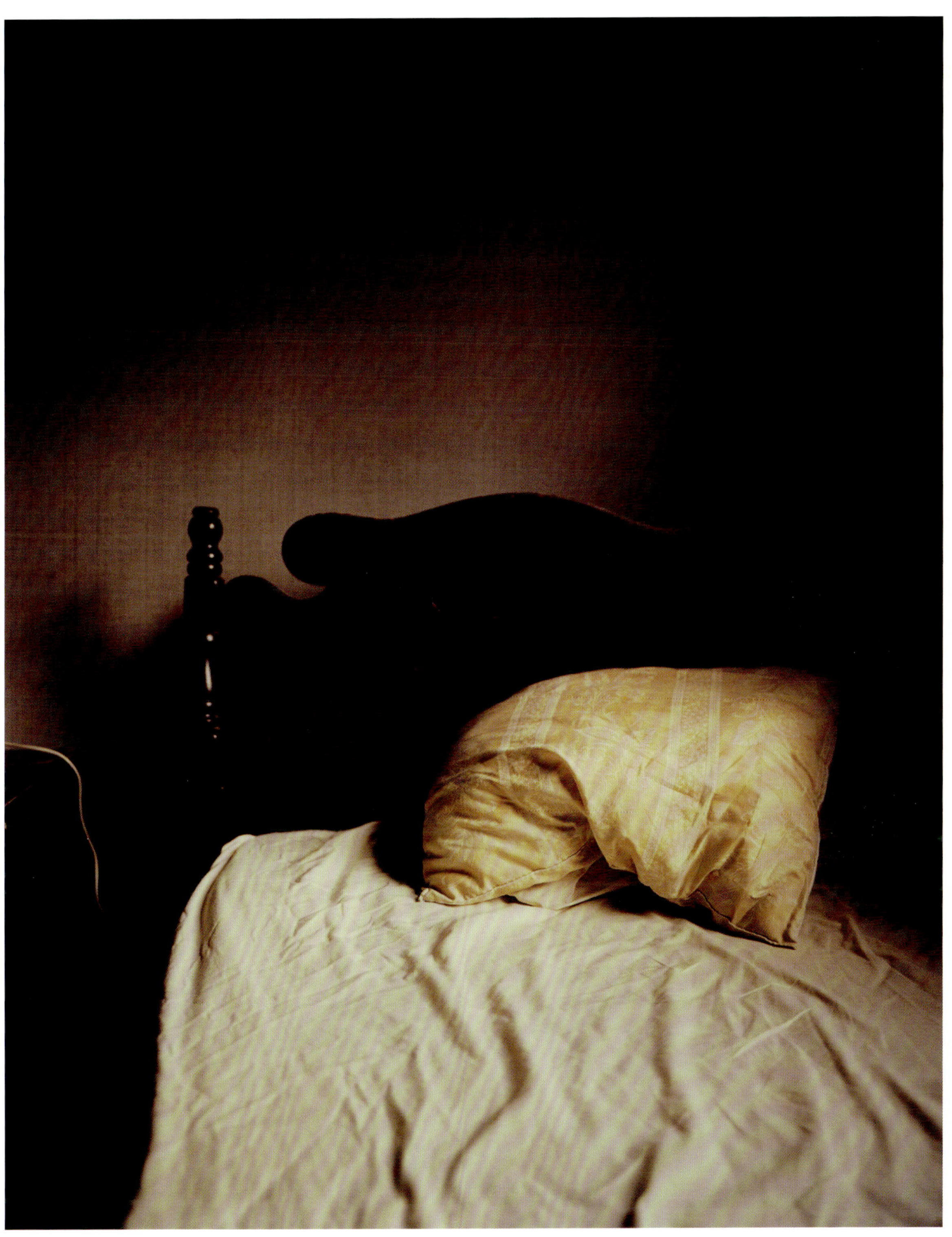

This picture of a bed has a very different meaning and feel to it. It's nighttime in a motel room. This is an adult bed and it has clearly been used—somebody was lying in that bed. The color sets the tone of this picture. That's the first thing you notice. The blue is both cold and melancholy, so the picture feels a bit off. You're not sure what's happened here. The real secret to color here, and one of the reasons why it's so odd, is that the picture was made in total darkness while the TV flickered. The only light source is television light, which casts a blue pallor on the white sheets. The walls were blue, but the TV made them a weirdly surreal set of blues. In the morning, in daylight, the room would look completely different. A space is transformed by when and how you choose to photograph it.

Walter Benjamin noted that Eugène Atget photographed Paris like it was a crime scene. I think about that when I walk into a room. I look for clues that tell me who may have been there and what may have happened. The walls do talk. Then I decide where to stand. I generally put the tripod in a place that shows as much of the room as I can get. I'm usually pressed against a wall holding my breath as I click the shutter so as not to knock the tripod during the exposure. As with the exteriors, practically nothing is photographed straight on. I purposely use the perspective of the room, which almost always leads to a corner that converges in the center of the picture. Those are the formal aspects of the image; the real story is in the marks, the light switches, the holes.

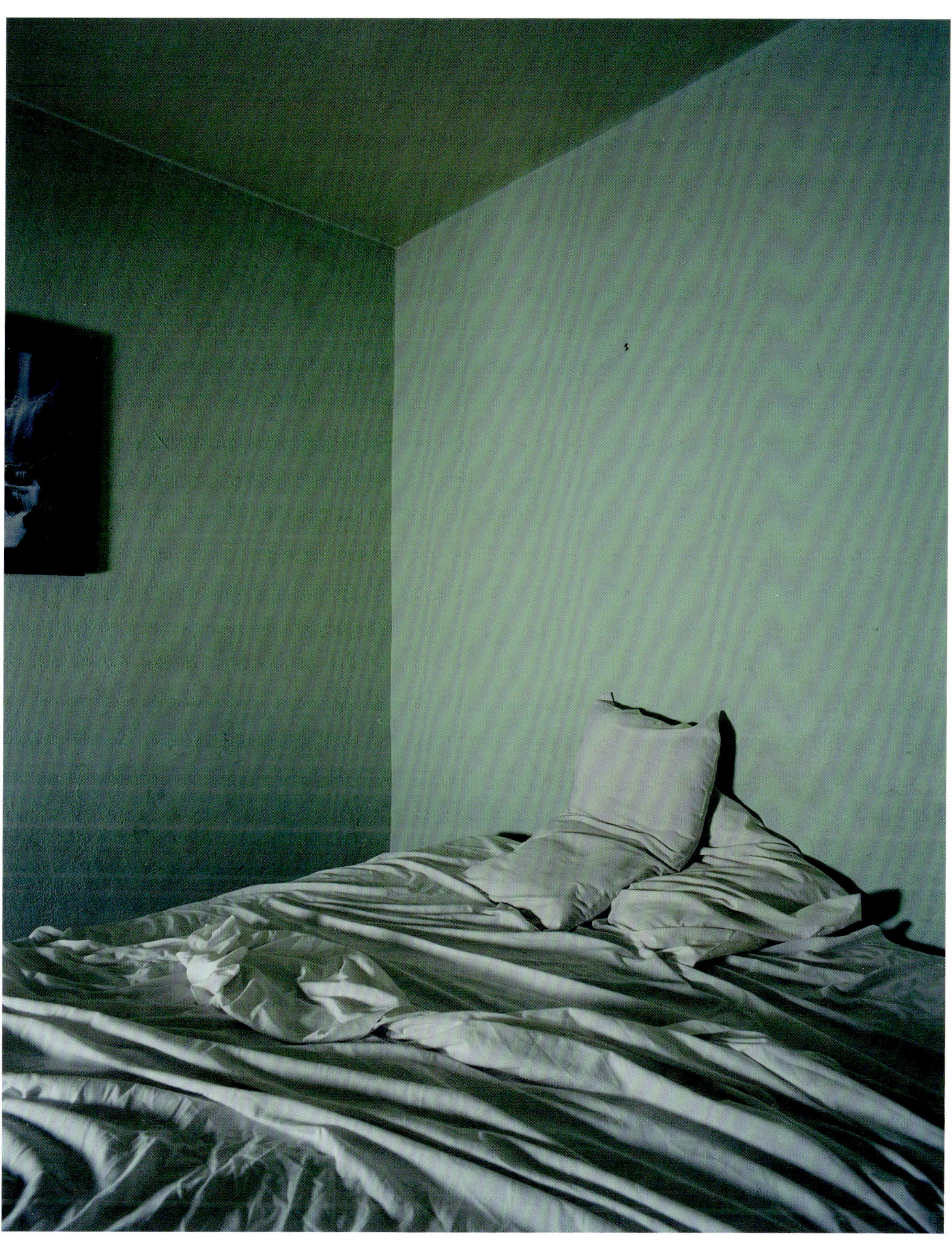

Todd Hido
#3878

What I See and What It Means

I don't analyze my photographs like this while I'm shooting. Making and analyzing are completely different processes.

You do have to examine things a little bit when you're making—there is some conscious recognition in wanting to take a picture—but as much as you can you should just make. See, respond, click. And the more you click, probably the better.

 Much of what happens in a picture is subconscious at the time I make it. I'm really seeing what's there later, when the picture is done. Joan Didion puts it this way, "I write entirely to find out what I'm thinking, what I see, and what it means. What I want and what I fear." I feel the same way about photography. I learn things from my work about what I'm thinking. My mind is way more sophisticated than I realize. Sometimes, I pull things out of my hat while I'm working and later I think, "Whoa, where did that come from?" Like when I saw the chair propped against the door and made the connection to issues of security. The act of photographing can bring inner things to the surface. I'll look at my pictures when they're finished and realize they are really touching on something deeper. One of the great pleasures of making photographs is being surprised by the results.

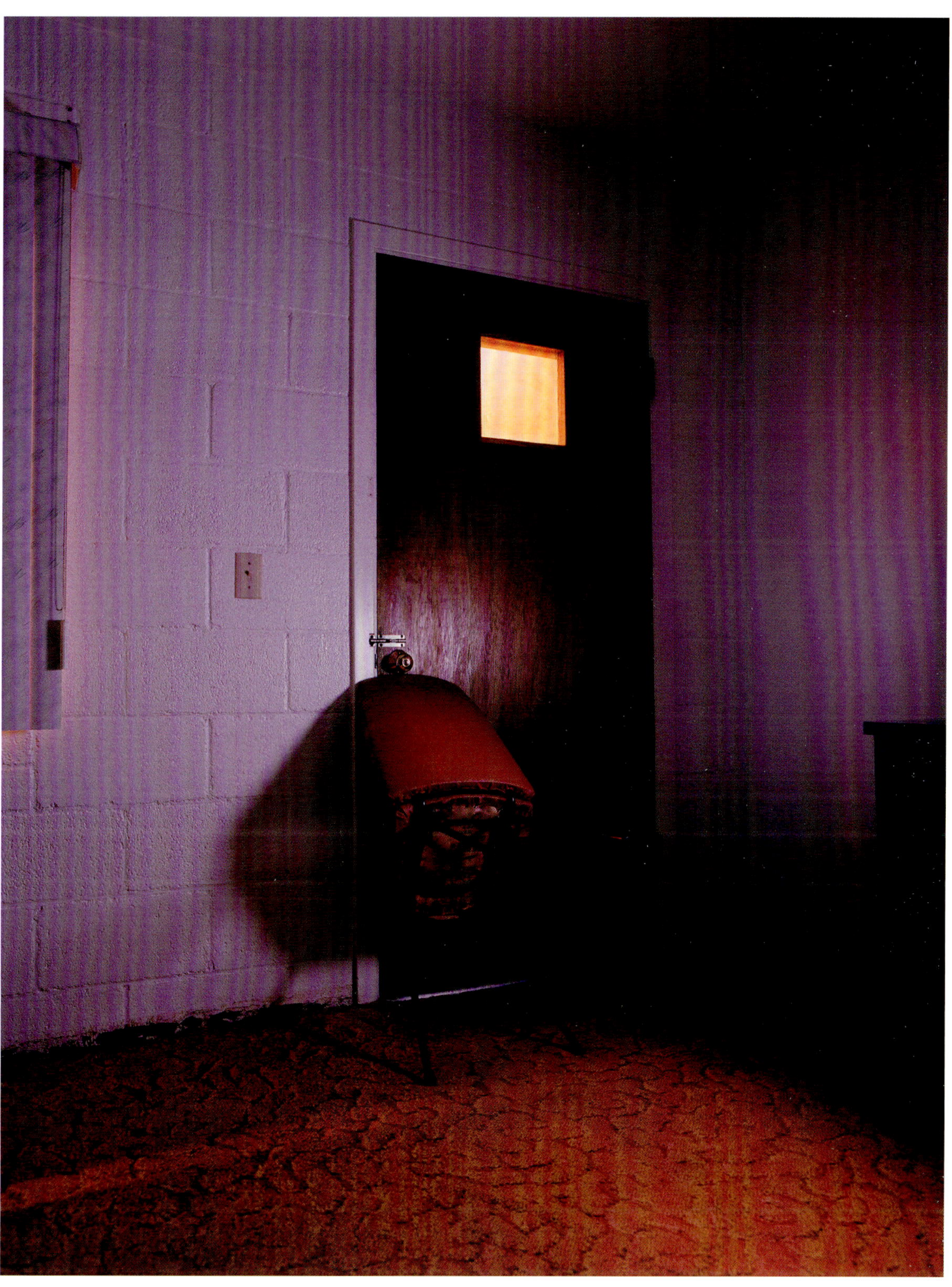

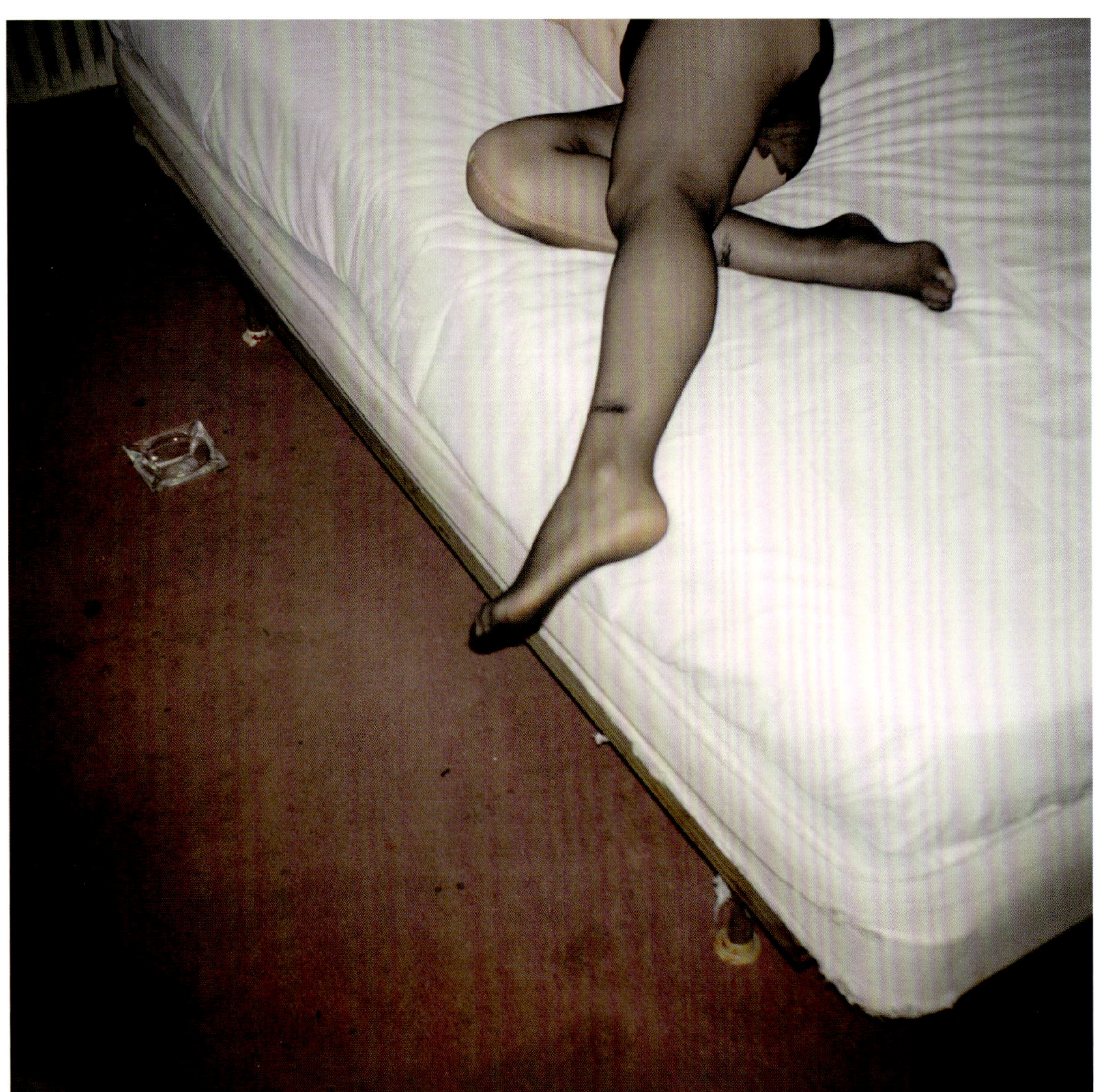

Just because I take a picture doesn't mean that somebody has to see it. Much of the time, the whole idea is to make pictures that nobody will see.

There are so many pictures that when you snap the shutter, that's the end of their existence. It's done. It never comes to life. You see it on a contact sheet, and you don't even look twice. The good pictures all have a certain power or electricity to them. For a picture to have a long life, it has to speak to me, have some meaning for me. And then of course, I hope it contains enough space to hold a range of meanings for others. You might have to take ten thousand frames to produce five hundred really good pictures.

When you see my work in a book or an exhibition or a presentation, it may seem tightly organized and rigorously consistent. But that's not representative of my day-to-day life as a working artist. If you look at my contact sheets, I am all over the place, as are most photographers really. If I see something I like, I take a picture, and that takes me down many different paths at the same time. The organization of one's work comes later. You have to just shoot and know you'll figure how it all comes together later.

Complicating the Story

After I had been making landscapes and interiors for a while, I felt like it was a natural progression to include people, to complicate the stories of home. I'd made portraits before but never really nudes. I liked the challenge of learning to work with a new subject matter. When I started photographing nudes, I felt like a beginner again, which was really exciting.

I started by photographing my friends, to get my style down. I knew I liked an empty space, and I knew that I liked window light. Then I started to run out of friends to photograph.

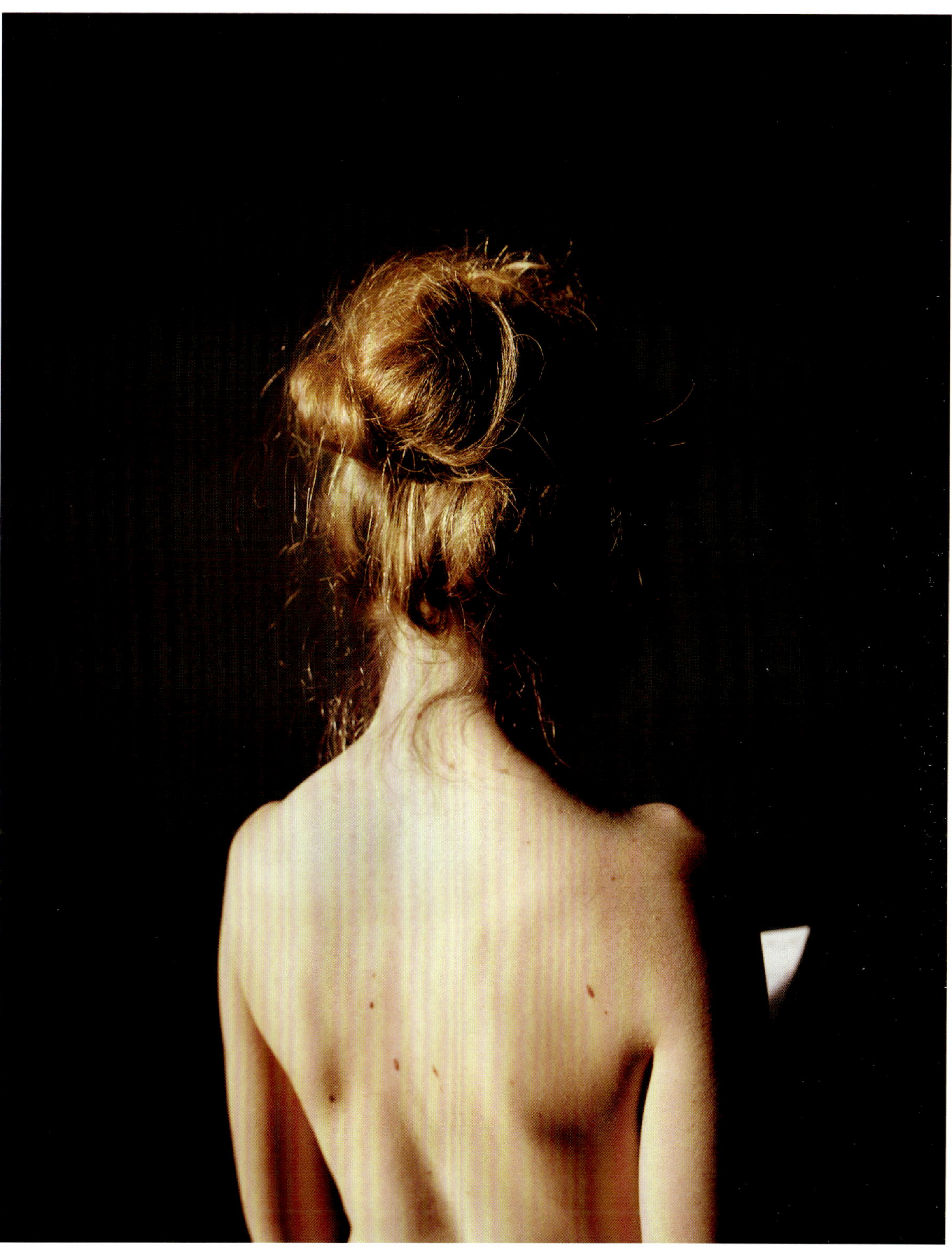

Todd Hido
#8869

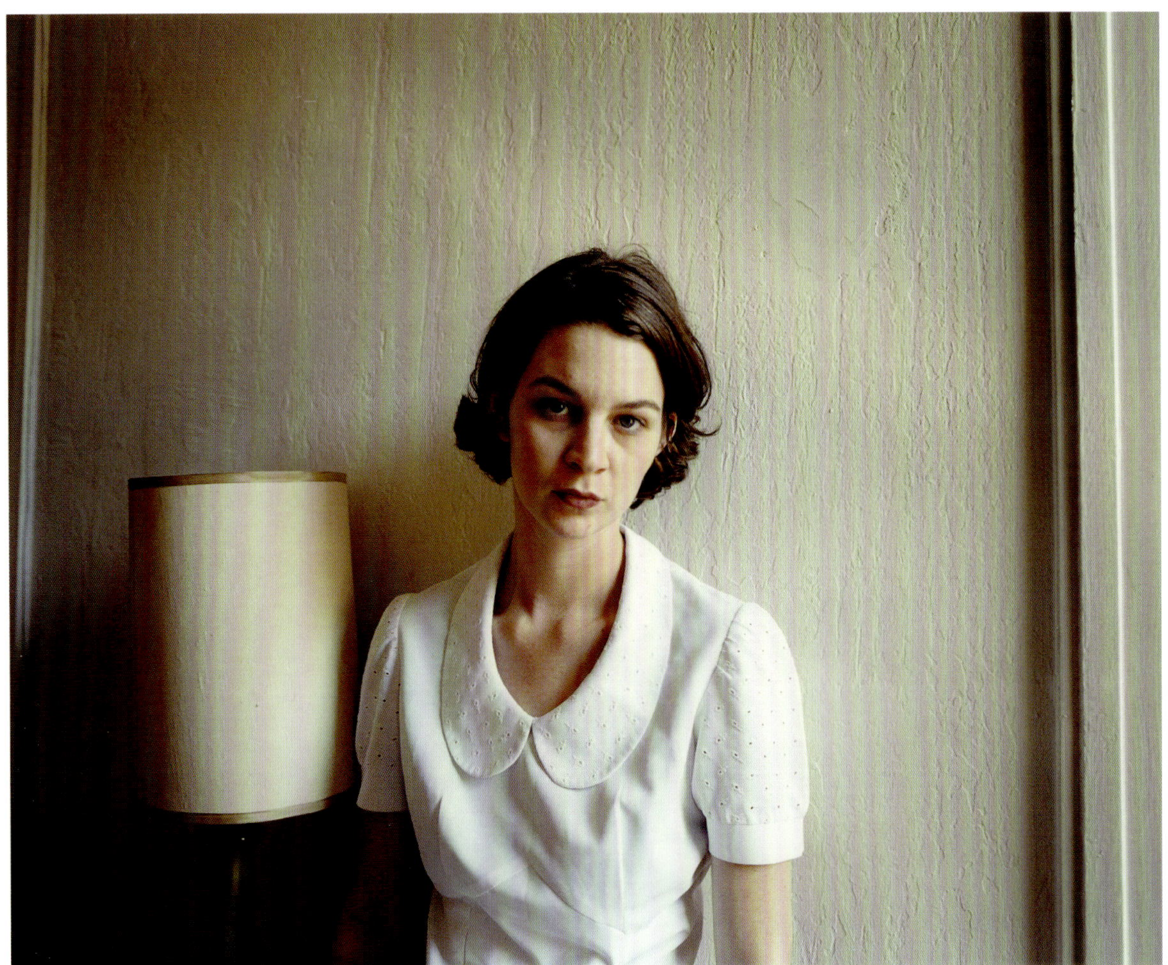

Any time you're working with a person as a subject, be it a portrait or a nude, very simple gestures become fascinating. You don't need to go for grand poses; subtle hand gestures and expressions of the eyes and mouth say it all. We are such complex communicators with our bodies that the slightest movement can alter the meaning of a picture. If a person lowers or raises their eyes, it changes everything.

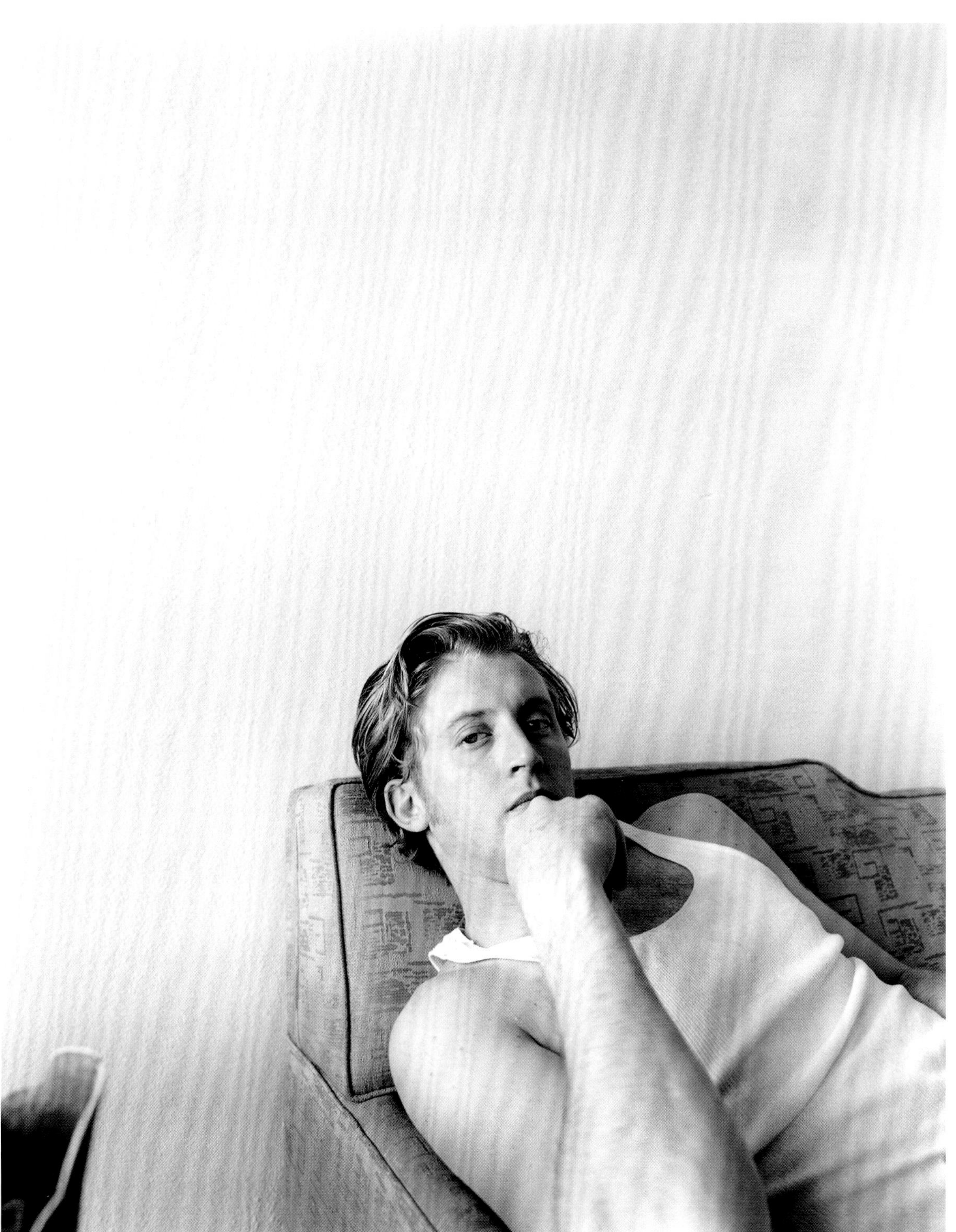

Todd Hido
#1427

81

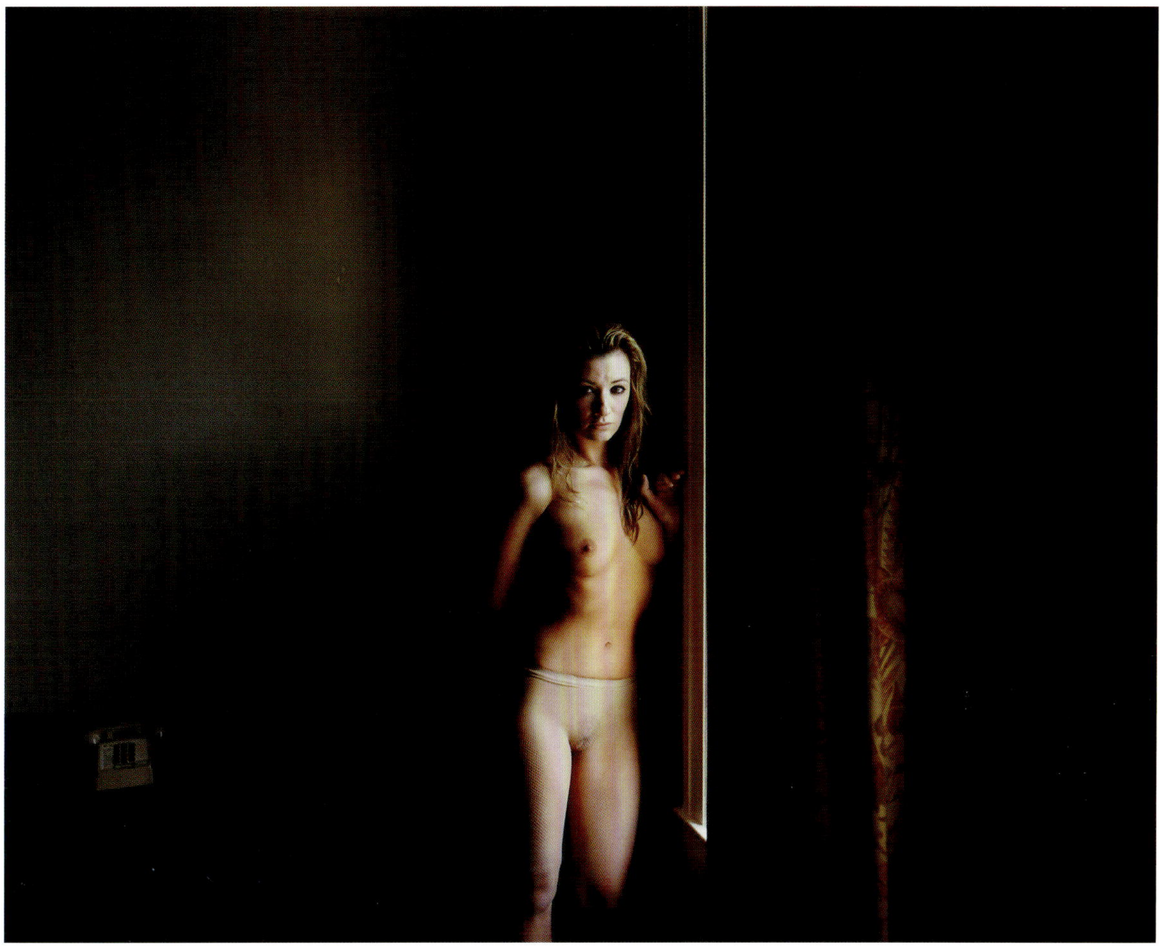

When I'm working with nude subjects, I'm looking for emotion—both theirs and mine. Whatever emotion may be there, or whatever emotion may arise during the process, people act a certain way when they're nude; there's an openness and a vulnerability that you just don't get otherwise.

When I'm trying to find people to photograph, I've noticed that there's a cast of characters that I already have built from and into my memory. There's this ineffable quality; it's like trying to describe why you love a certain person or why you are attracted to one person over another. Though I don't think I choose my models based on attraction. It's not about anything that reductive. In an odd way, it comes back to surfaces. When I'm photographing people, the kind of person they are in reality isn't relevant. It doesn't matter if they are nice or mean or funny or cool for the picture. They're an actor, a stand-in for a person or situation from my history. So I'm immediately able to divorce myself from any need to record them as they are. I'm not like Bruce Davidson in East 100th Street, photographing people to whom I might have some responsibility to tell their story faithfully. I don't need to do that. What I'm interested in is making a picture that speaks to me, that tells me my own story in a new way.

Nudes and Narrative

The nude has been pictured extensively in the history of photography. I wanted to make nudes that were different from what had been done before. I don't always care about that, but in this case I thought about contributing to the field, instead of just working with nudes. I feel like some of the pictures approach that.

I've never done a "nude in nature" shot. It would never occur to me to put a person on the beach or on a rock as a form. I love the work of Edward Weston, and he photographed that perfectly. It's been done, and even if it had not been done, I wouldn't have been interested. Capturing the formal aspects of the body isn't what I'm after. For me, it's the relationship the nude has to a particular place. Why is a nude in this bedroom? What is happening?

By simply putting a person and a place together, a story is activated. I've always loved the illustrations on the covers of pulp fiction novels. The pictures are so enticing because they're filled with implied narrative; they convey a strong sense of the whole story without giving it away—in one picture. It's very difficult to do that. Those covers are a big influence on how I photograph nudes. I'm trying to raise questions about what might be happening outside the frame and inside the story.

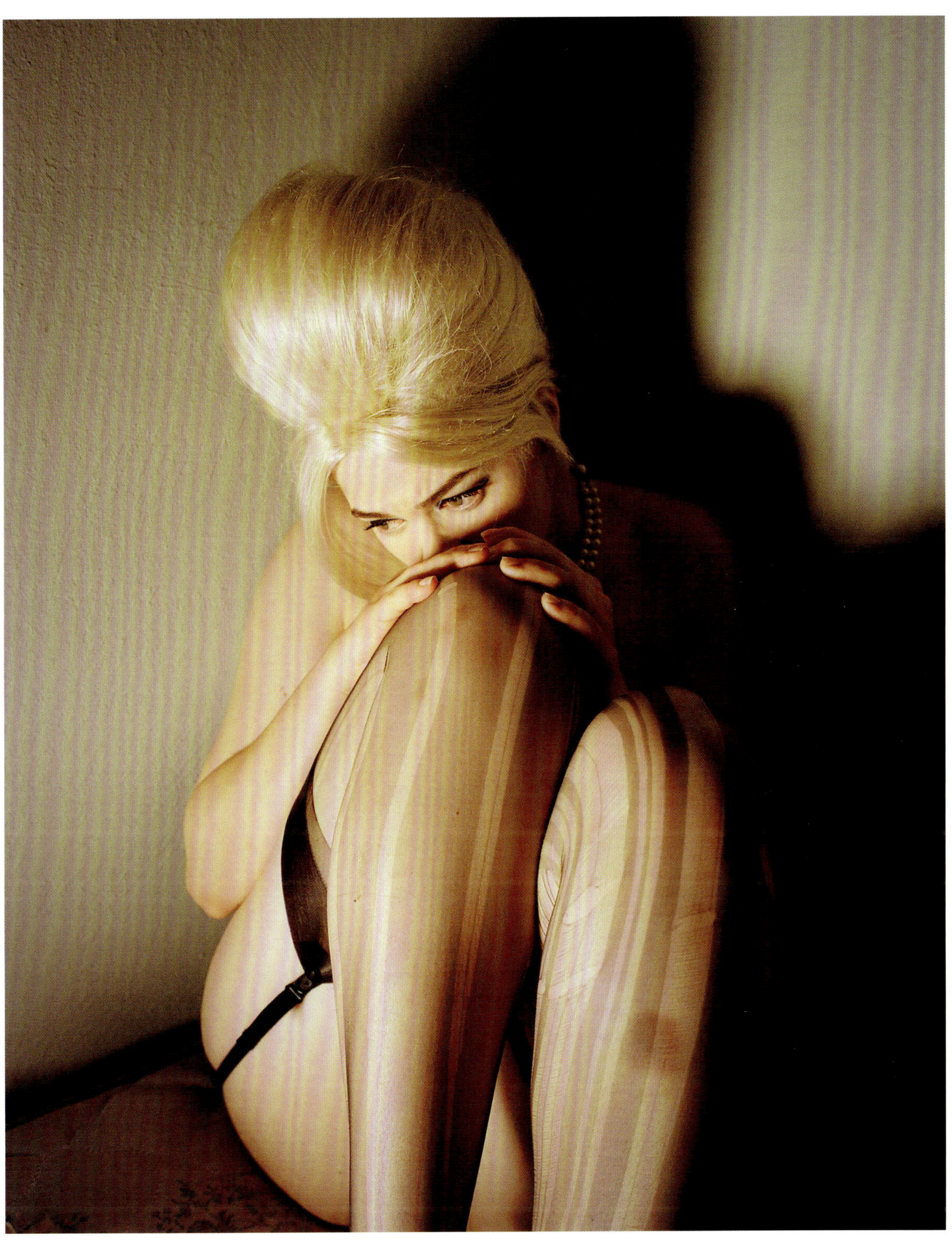

Todd Hido
#10479-11a

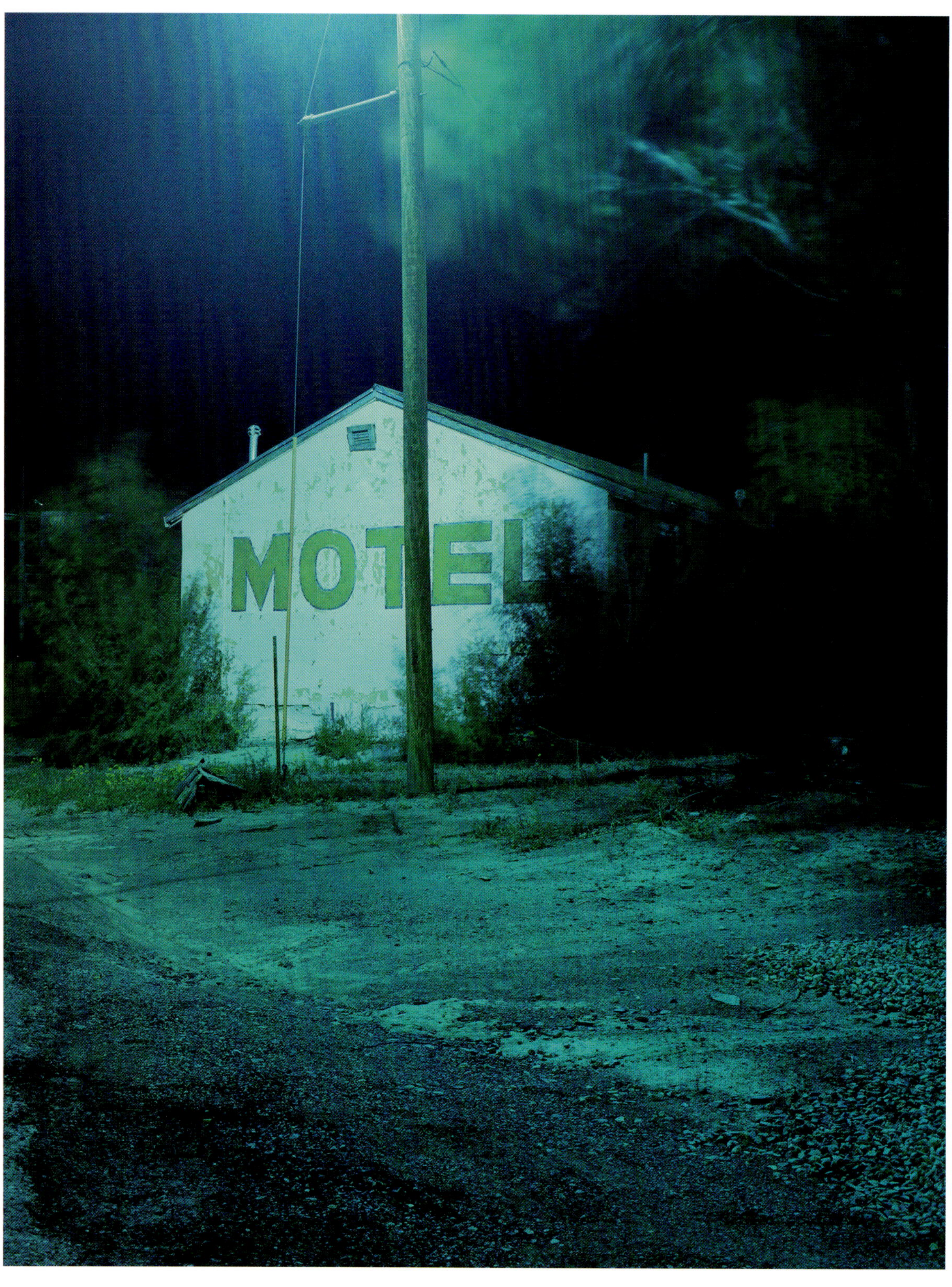
MOTEL

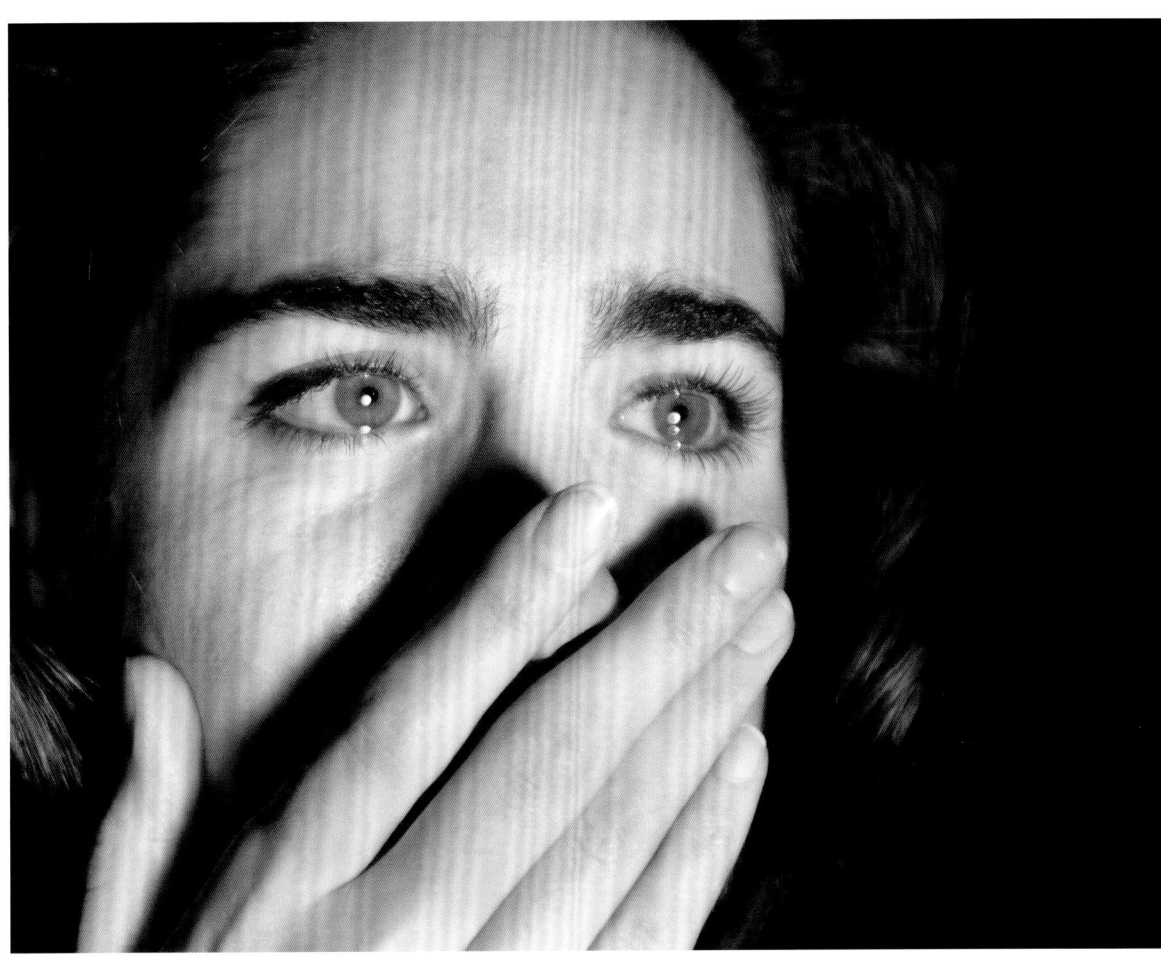

When I'm taking pictures of people, I usually have a loose storyline in mind. Every portrait that you take is constructed in some way, unless you're walking down the street and taking a candid shot, like Garry Winogrand. Pictures are only unconstructed as long as the person doesn't see you. When the person sees the photographer, it's not candid anymore.

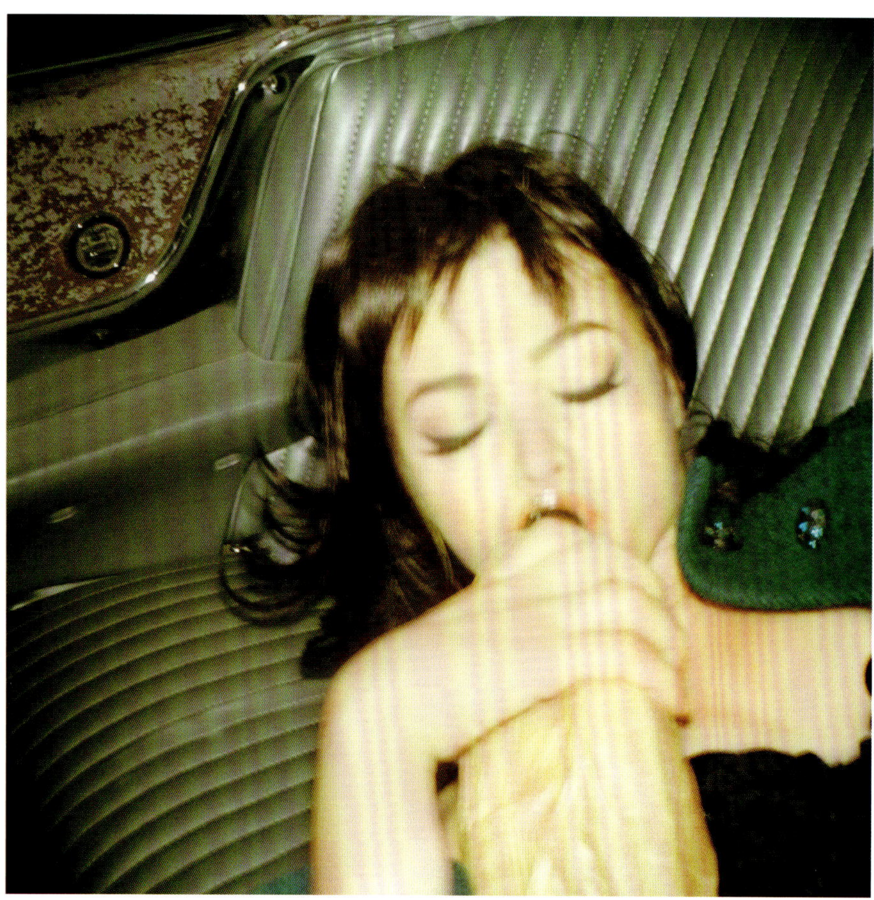

Some of these pictures of women relate to my traumatic childhood. I've seen things that a boy shouldn't see. The woman above is sort of a stand-in for someone in my past. It isn't always that concrete, but most of the photographs are set in the past. This half-pulp fiction, half-reality image in which a woman gets drunk and then loose in the back of a car reflects some of my own experiences.

I tend to photograph what's occupying my mind, the thoughts that keep me up at night. I photograph things that trouble me in some way, like relationship turmoil—in the way you wouldn't write about how great everything is in your journal.

I don't always understand what the work means to me when I'm making it. I'm still in the thick of it. If I knew the answers to all the questions, especially the deeper more internal ones, then I would have moved on already. You don't have to know the answers; you don't always need a clear-cut thesis. Sometimes the reason you're working on something only makes sense to you years later.

The picture above right is of my mom, for real, in the '70s, and the picture below it is of a model I work with a lot, Khrystyna. You can see that she and my mother look very similar. These pictures are staged and they're fiction, but there's something of the truth at the heart of them.

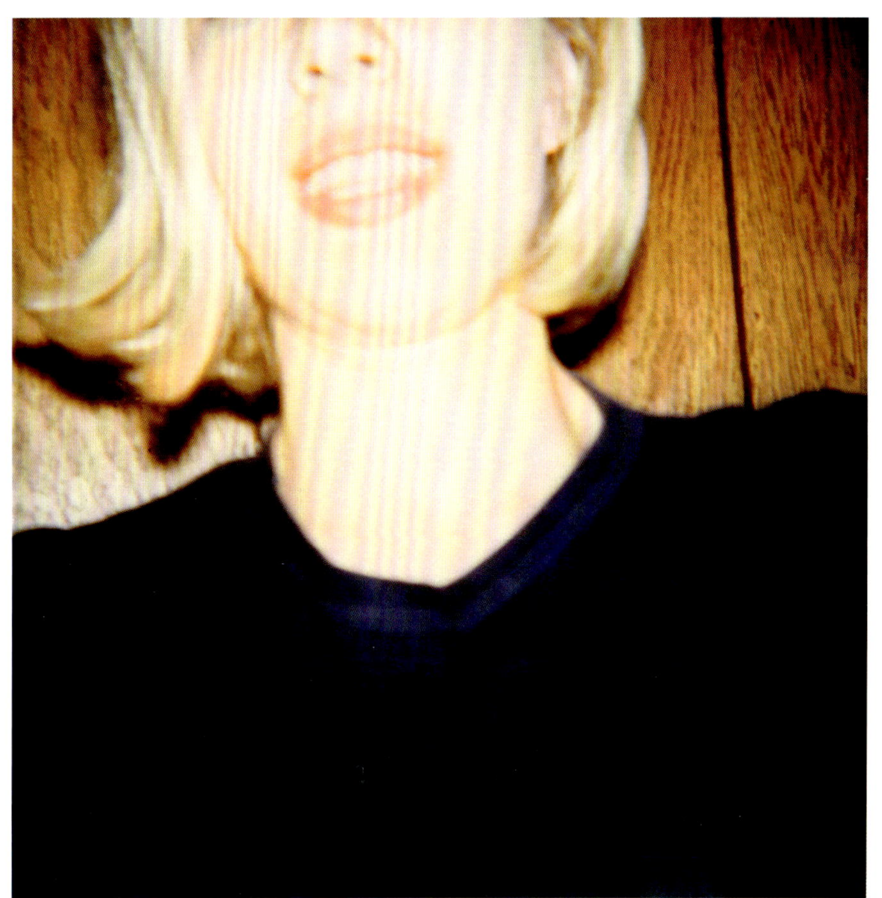

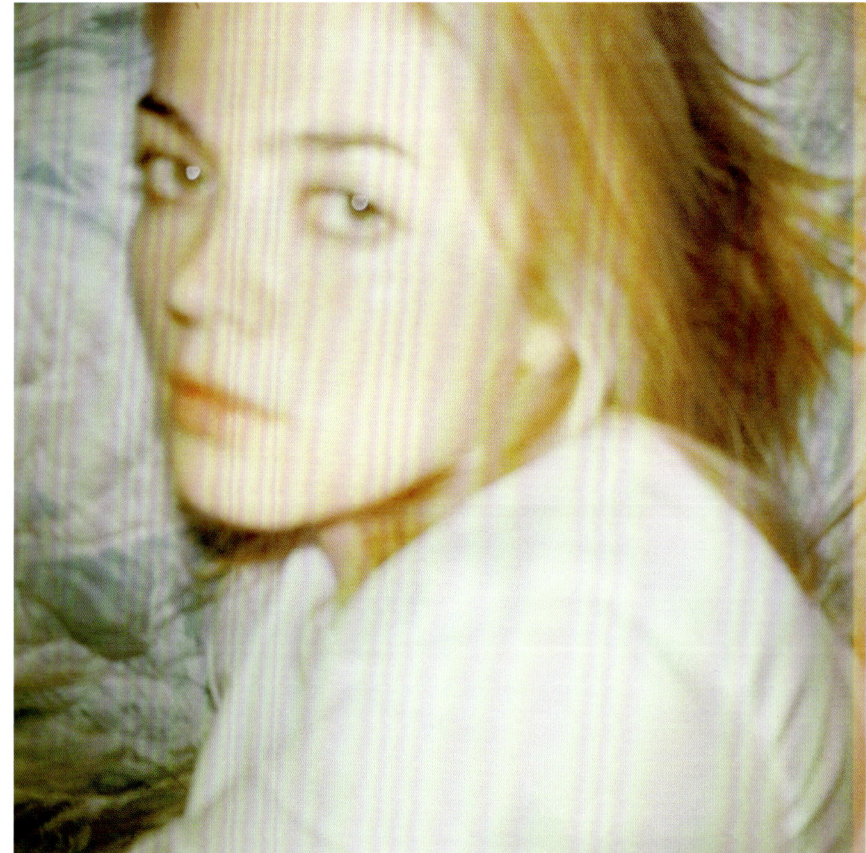

Left
Todd Hido
#10573-a

Above
Todd Hido
#2399

Right
Todd Hido
#9485-a

What Is True

I think there's real value as an artist in working with the same person over time. It's similar to shooting in the same place, to "finding a place you trust and trusting it for a while." I've made great growth in the complexity of what I'm able to explore and express in my art by working with Khrystyna. There is something that unites us in our histories though she grew up in Siberia and I grew up in Ohio. Something back there in our minds just clicks. We don't talk about it. We just take pictures.

Khrystyna is not afraid to look ugly or be in a compromising, weird position; she'll be that character. But then she turns into Marilyn Monroe. In other pictures, she's Debbie Harry. She has the ability to resemble these characters and types. I'm not always trying for these looks. I just recognize when to take the picture.

When you're consistently working with a model, a kind of safe space for you and for them to be vulnerable develops. The models know that I'm not there because something physical between us is going to happen. So it becomes a space for other things to be acted out. They feel comfortable projecting for the camera, and I feel comfortable exploring that projection without the pressures of reality.

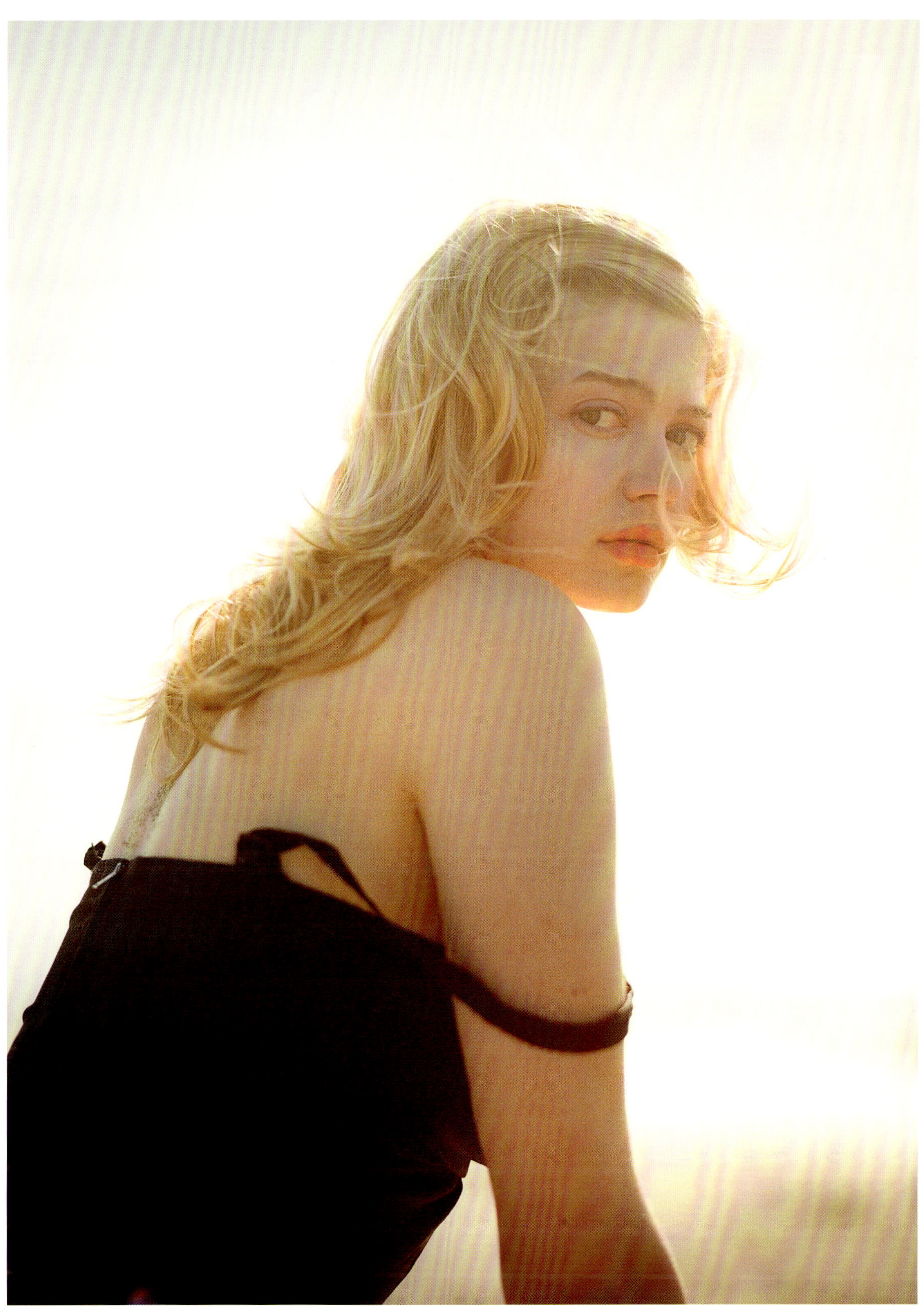

Todd Hido
#11250-09

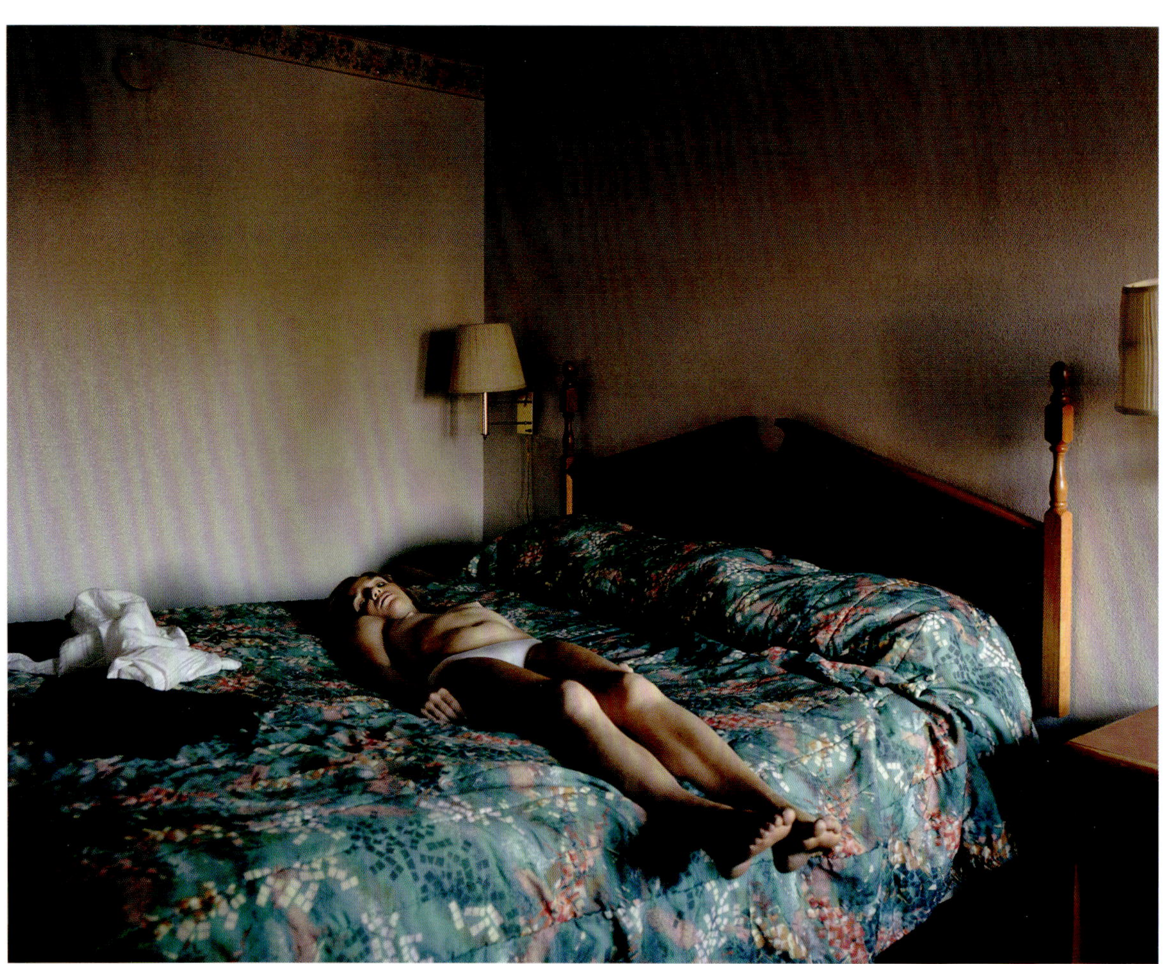

You can create a fiction, but maybe you're telling a story that's real in the end.

Picasso once famously said, "Give a man a mask, and he'll tell you the truth." I think that happens with my work. These are real stories: mine, a friend's, or a model's. Sometimes they are stories that I hear on the news.

That's one of the gifts of the medium. The camera is a magical machine that can record something that's completely true, and at the same time, a total lie—simply by stopping time at the wrong moment. Subjects might look like they're crying when they're laughing, or look drunk when they just have their eyes closed. The point is, photography can describe everything in the frame in great detail, but the meaning of what's described is ambiguous.

Whether the photograph is true or not doesn't matter. What matters is what you want to say as an artist to the world, even if the meaning eludes you too. It's engaging to purposely make a picture in which the truth is slippery, that resists a definitive meaning, that stays in the zone of "is it real, is it not real?" I like to work in that zone.

What Prevails

At home, I have a TV on that is playing CNN twenty-four hours a day. I like to have white noise in the background, and I hear all kinds of crazy stories reported because the world is messed up. These background stories influence the scenarios that I'm fictionalizing. They creep into my work and thoughts.

Dorothea Lange said that a photographer should concentrate on what "exists and prevails." I thought about that for a long time. At first, I dismissed it as something meant only for documentary photographers. And then I realized that my work, when it is a fiction and when it's not, is about what exists and prevails in our culture too.

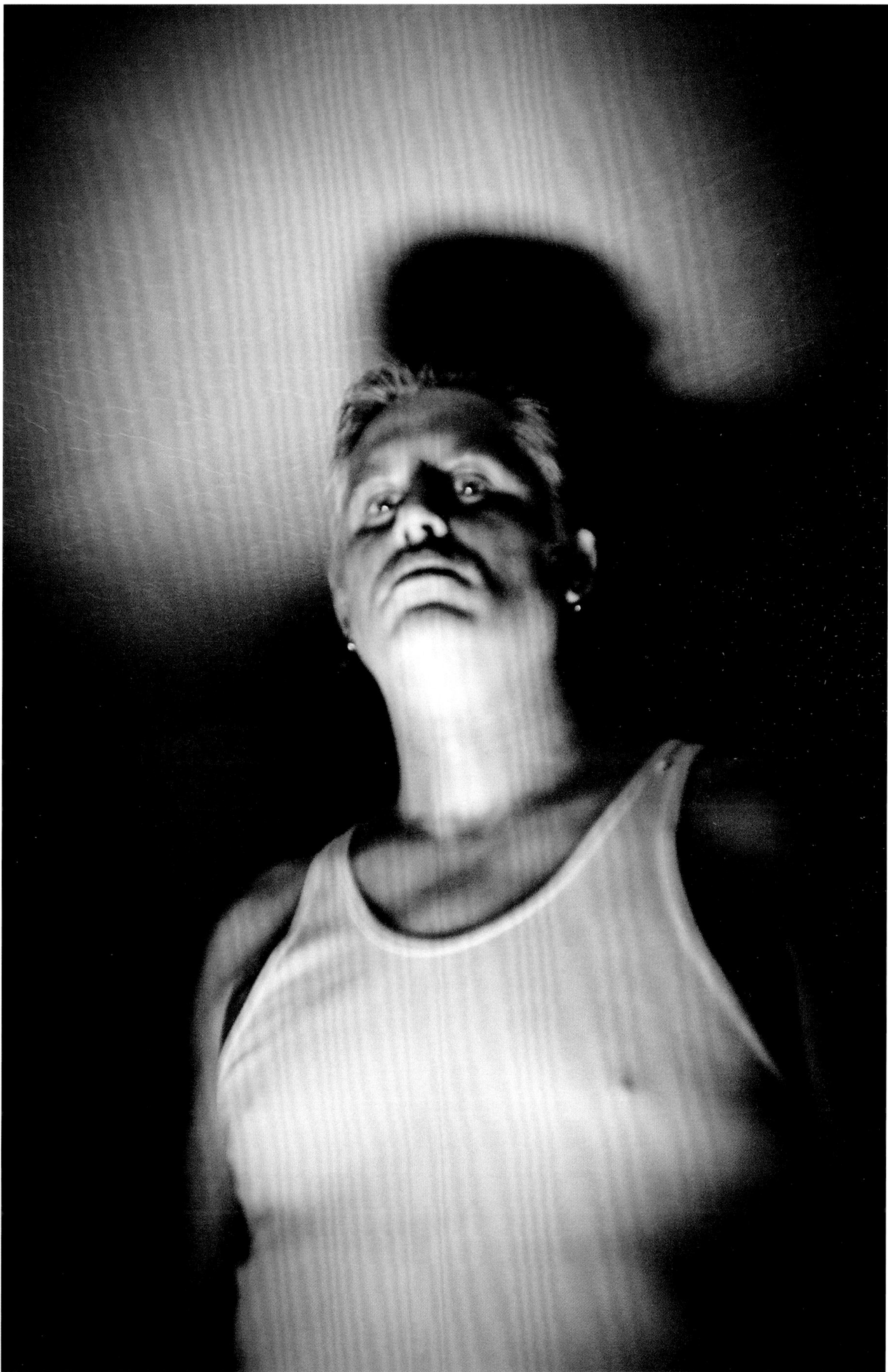

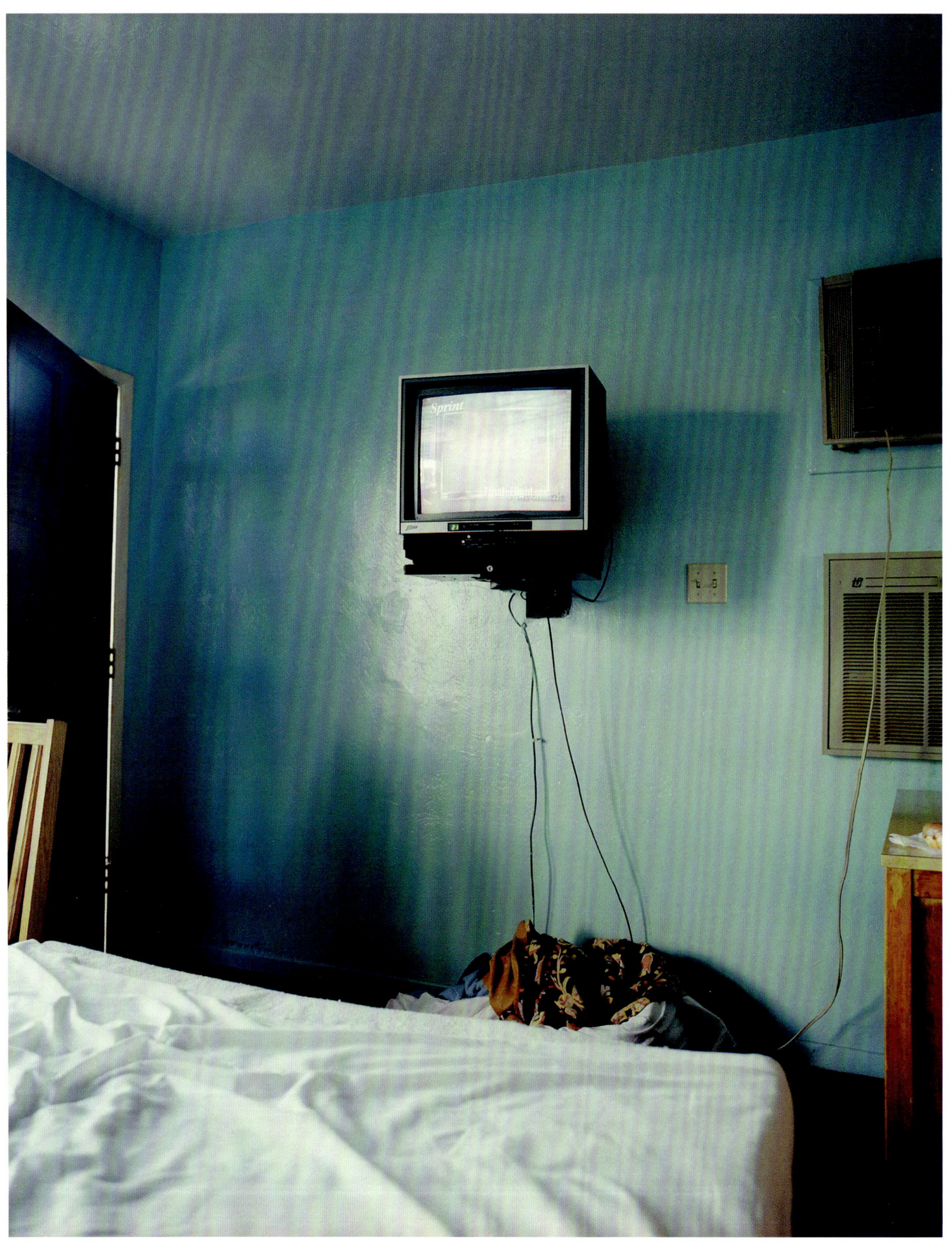

Sprint

Setting the Stage

I set the stage for a picture to occur. I always make sure that I have the location nailed down. I like the scene to be kind of sparse so that you can really focus on the subject. A lot of times I work in hotel rooms, and the first thing I do is strip the bedspread off the bed to get rid of that funky pattern and make it blank. The bed also looks more used then.

You can have an amazing story to tell, but you have to get the setting right. Location is everything. The place is part of the story, and the details are crucial. If the place isn't right, it doesn't matter what's going on in the picture. When you're shooting a portrait of somebody, if you don't have the right background, or if you haven't moved the stuff out of the way that isn't part of the story, the photograph is not going to convey what you're trying to say. When I'm shooting, all I see at first are the potential errors in the background; I can't even see the person until I fix all that.

I set up a situation in a space that gives it context, so that the characters can do something natural within it. In that way, pictures are only partially staged. The characters do the rest.

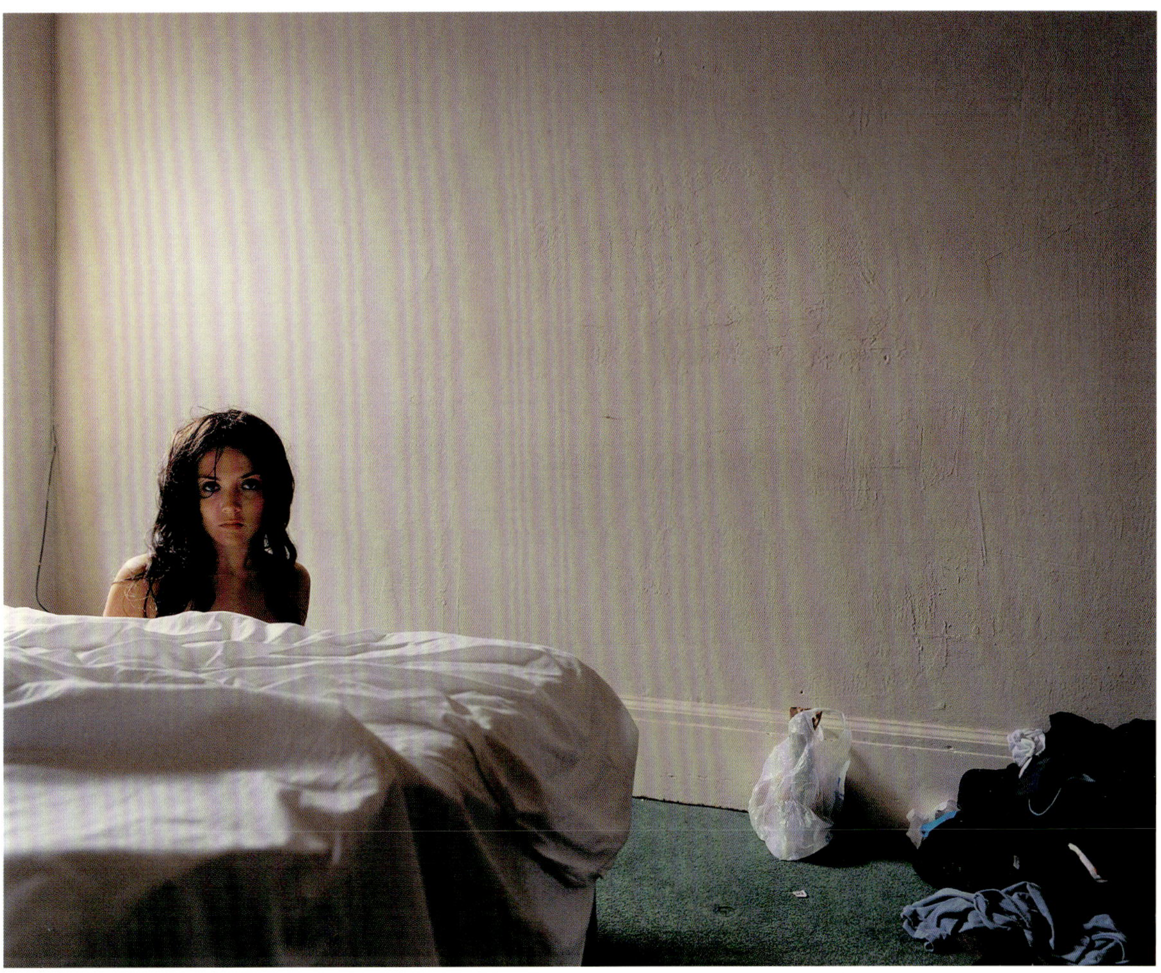

One of the things I learned from Frederick Sommer is that if you're trying to make a still life and you arrange every part of it, it's not going to be any good. The same could be said about a portrait. You have to create an environment where random things can still occur and then recognize when to take the picture. Things can very easily look contrived or self-conscious within a photograph. If you predetermine everything that will happen in front of you, the photograph will look too particular.

So you set the stage so something natural and unanticipated can occur. Then the picture will have an authenticity to it and that is really important. I don't like things that look super-staged. I find images more compelling when things are more gritty and realistic. I don't care if you stage it, just don't make it look staged.

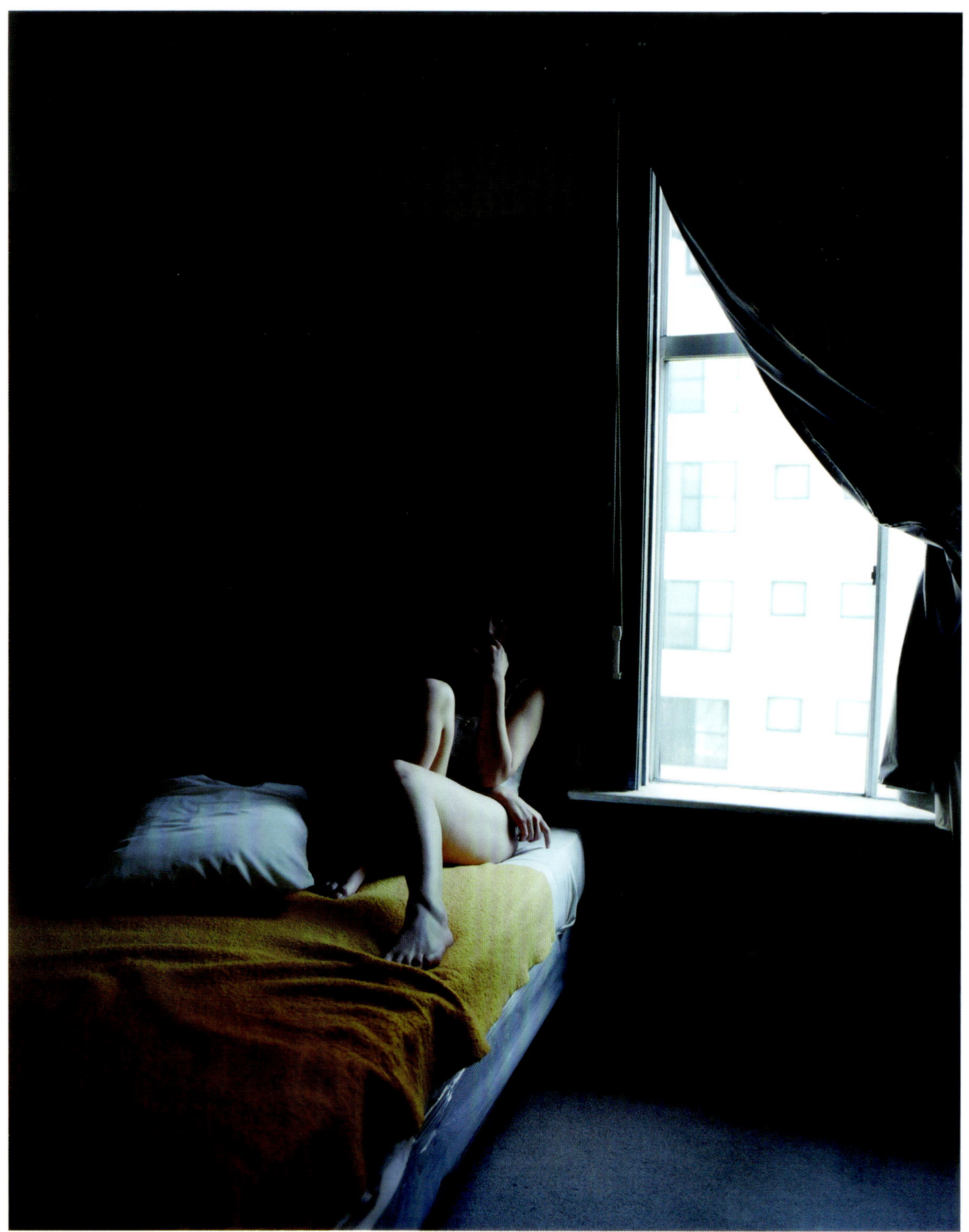

The Authentic Moment

Everybody's seen a fashion shoot on TV. That way of shooting and posing, I've found, produces contrived-looking results. Models often have these ideas about the way a photography shoot should work: they're supposed to pose, and it goes fast, and blah, blah, blah. You have to get around this perception when you're working with models in order to shoot something more authentic. If you, as the photographer, just stand there and don't do anything, it can get really awkward, because they think that they're not doing well. If you're not snapping, you're silently saying, "No, I don't like that."

What I do in this situation is let people pose and do their thing for a while. If the model poses, I snap; if she moves, I snap. If you keep that snapping going, there's a flow that happens. Click, click, click. Eventually, you click the posing out of them. And then, you say, "I've got to change my film or check my ISO. Hold on a second." When you pause like this, they stop being "America's Next Top Model" and relax for a second. And that's when you get the real picture.

There's a really wonderful Avedon photograph of Marilyn Monroe taken in one of these in-between moments. It's one of my favorite photos of all time. The story behind the picture is that when Monroe said, "Are we on?" Avedon said, "No." And that's when Avedon snapped the picture. In that moment she didn't have her guard up—she doesn't have her happy face on, she isn't being an actress, she is just a person who is lost inside her soul.

A Distant Intimacy

As with my other work, I'm consciously deciding where to stand in these photographs. I move around to different spots. A lot of times, I'm across the bed from the subject. This establishes a certain distance and helps place the viewer in the space. Just because you're in a room with somebody who is nude doesn't mean it's an intimate situation. Sometimes, it's awkward, and I let that become part of the picture. Where I stand emphasizes emotional distance even though there's physical proximity. In many ways the photographs are the opposite of my landscapes, which feel intimate though they cover far more distance.

In this image, my stance takes prominence. The picture is very tense and uncomfortable. The woman is clearly vulnerable. The camera is directly over her, representing the person who has got her down. In some ways, I'm standing in my dad's position, recreating a moment that I witnessed, but from his perspective. The camera allows the photographer to become different people, to look at situations from different perspectives.

I think of this as a kind of "remastering." When you've had a bad experience, you sometimes feel compelled to recreate it in a way that allows you to control it. It's like you're attracted to the very thing that bothered you because you're not done with it—you need to fix that moment so you can move forward. Oscar Wilde said, "A burnt child loves the fire." For me, that means being attracted to explore things that have been traumatic or that you're not so sure about. The sources of terror in childhood can become sources of attraction in adulthood. Or, in the case of an artist, inspiration.

Art is a good vehicle for figuring things out for yourself, a tool for walking through a situation in your mind that you keep separate from the anxieties of reality. There's something about making photographs that allows you to act out your story and make it visible.

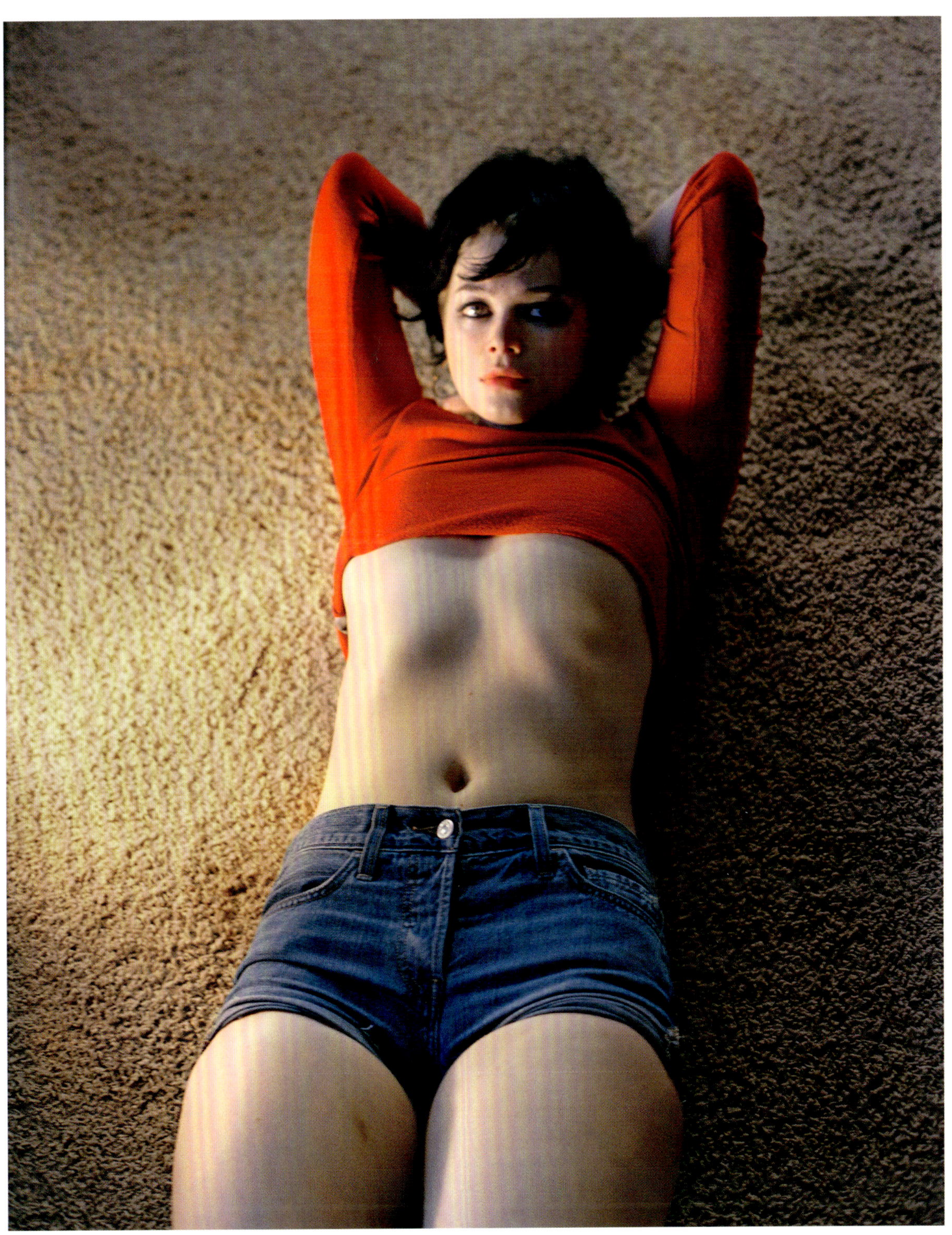

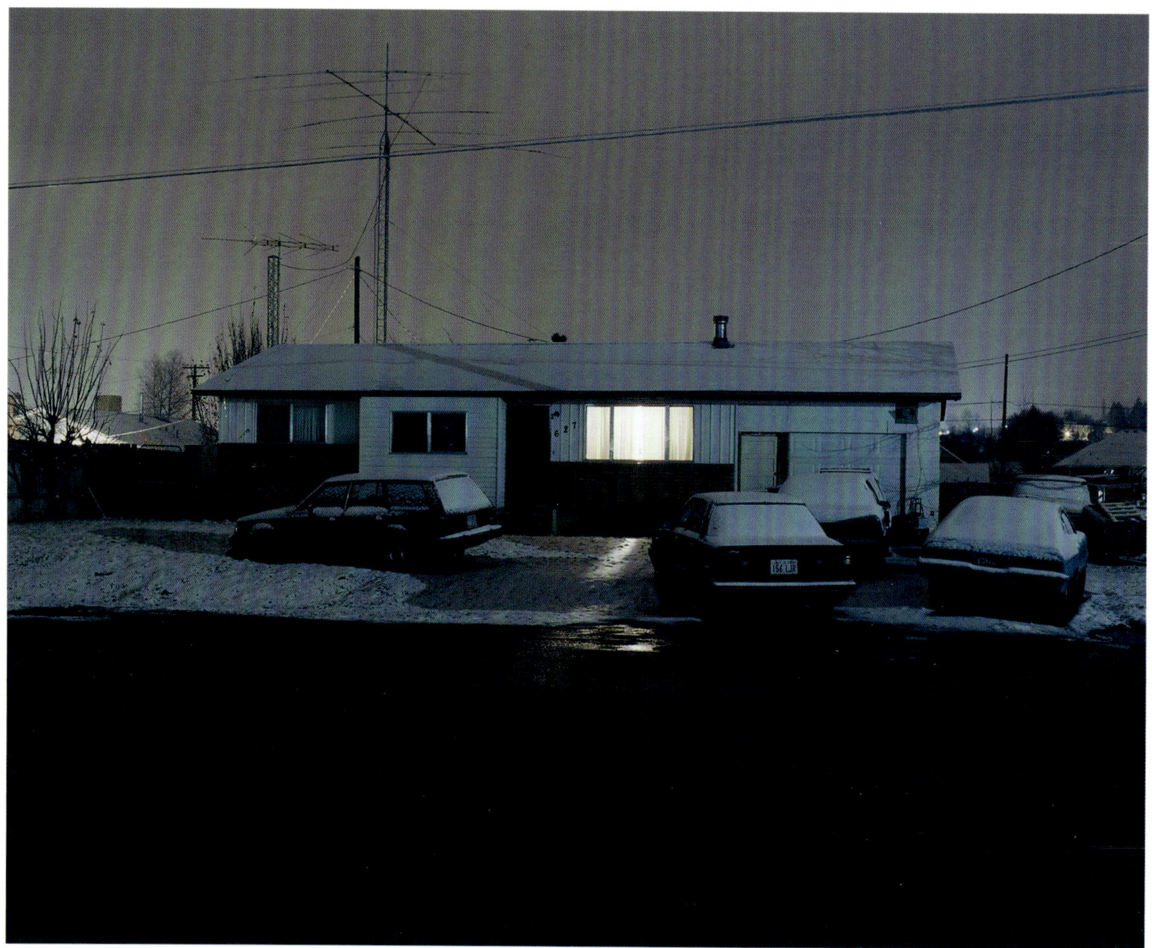

Building the Story

After a while, I had amassed all these pictures of people and they made sense
to me, but they needed to make sense to others. I needed to locate these women
within a larger context. In cinema, you would add in establishing shots before
meeting the characters, so it made sense to me to start combining the pictures
and mix the different genres together. I find that I really like what happens when
you pair a person with a place. It opens the door for more complex storytelling.

Over many years, I've started to think of what I'm doing as building an
archive of photographs to draw from to create stories. When it's time for a show
or a book, I go to that archive and look at everything that I haven't used before.
Usually, the newest pictures are my favorites, and I'll start to build from there,
putting them together with other older pictures. That's how my sequences originate.

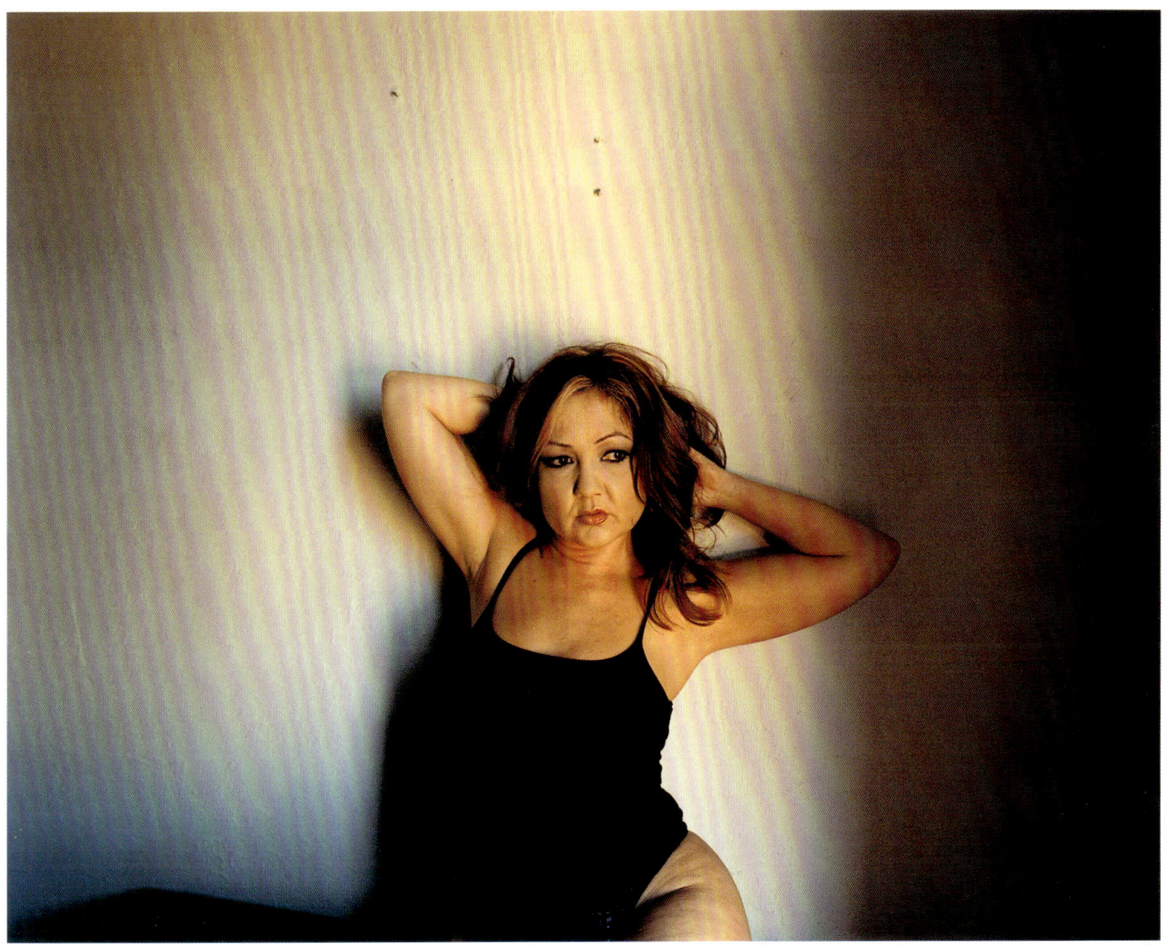

One of the most magical things about photography happens when you place one picture next to another picture to create new meanings. When you see a picture of a person and another of a place, your mind automatically fills in gaps as if they're connected. In a classic cinematic approach, you would go down a road, meet a character, and understand that's where she lives. And then in the next scene, you understand that the interior is inside that house. If I put a picture of the outside of a hotel with a picture of a woman on a bed—boom— I've given you enough material to create a story. If you take a picture of a rainy, cold, dark moment, and then put that picture next to a portrait, it will impact how that person is understood and will set the tone for understanding the situation. Something happens in the space between pictures when you string them together. They automatically set a narrative in motion in our minds.

It really doesn't take too many different components to create a narrative. There are three basic elements: person, place, emotion. Sometimes I'll supply actions or the aftermath of actions in my work. You can do almost anything with these few fundamental components. You can tell a really complicated story, and that's what I'm after. I've loaded the deck for meaning to occur.

Photographs are still so no action is ever taking place; whatever occurred happened in the past. Everything is presented and described but nothing actually happens in a photograph.

A movie doesn't simply describe things and not further its plot. Action unfolds in a movie. The still quality of photography makes it suitable for the kind of buildup to an event that isn't depicted—to open-ended scenes, the moment in a film when something is about to happen. The real story in photography happens outside the frame—in the gaps, and in the viewer's mind when they look at it.

I put pictures together to create these stories, but I'm aware that the series of photographs can't contain the whole story or even fully make sense. I think about Wim Wenders's *Wings of Desire* a lot. The angels fly from one scene to another, and the movie enters a person's life and story. You don't see what happens before or after. Then the angels fly somewhere else. When I was setting up a sequence of photographs for *Excerpts from Silver Meadows*, I thought about it as if I were ducking in and out of people's lives. I'll take the road to a place and we'll be there for a little bit, and then we'll go to somewhere else and be there for a short time, and then move on again. This formed the shape and structure of that body of work.

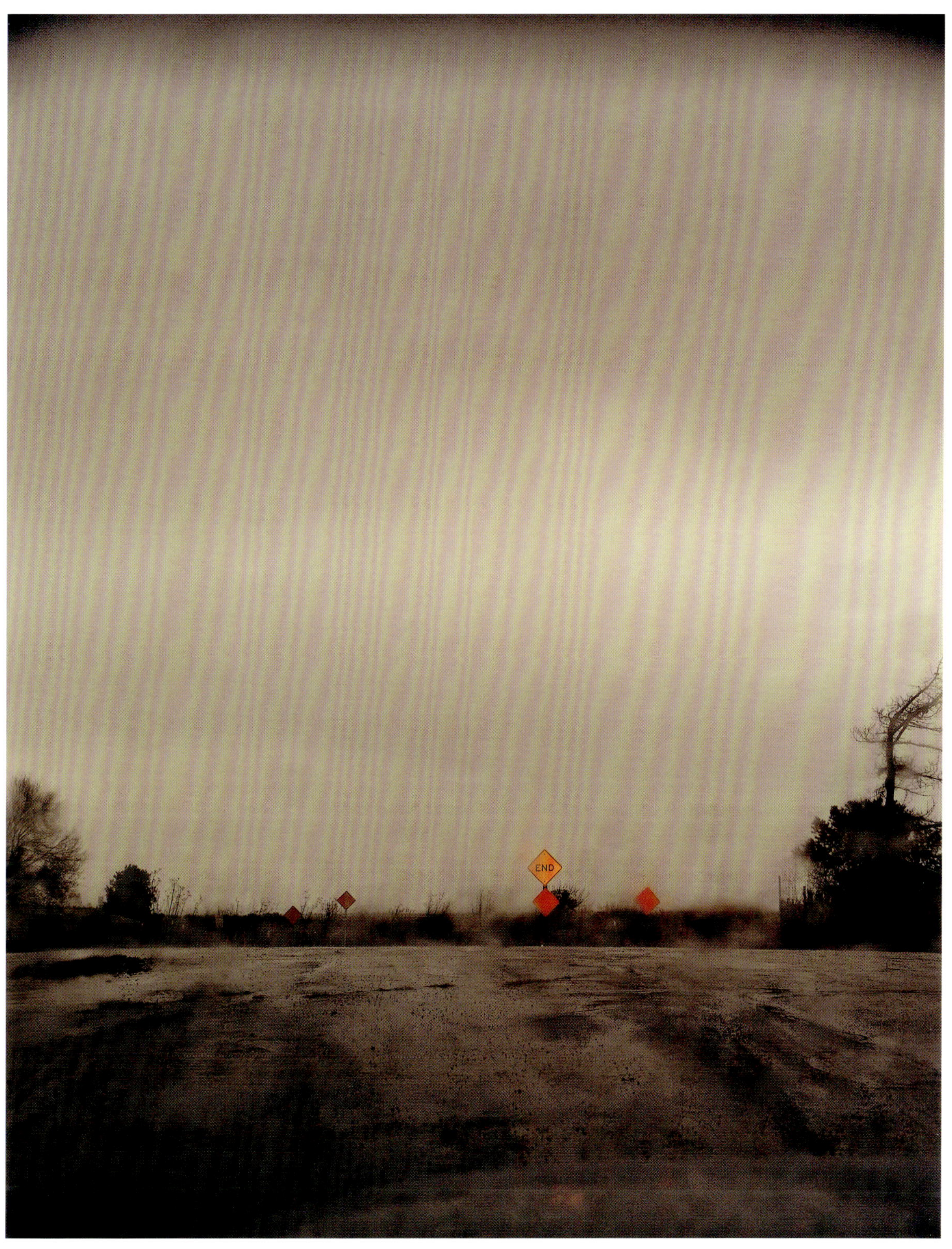

Todd Hido
#4155-a

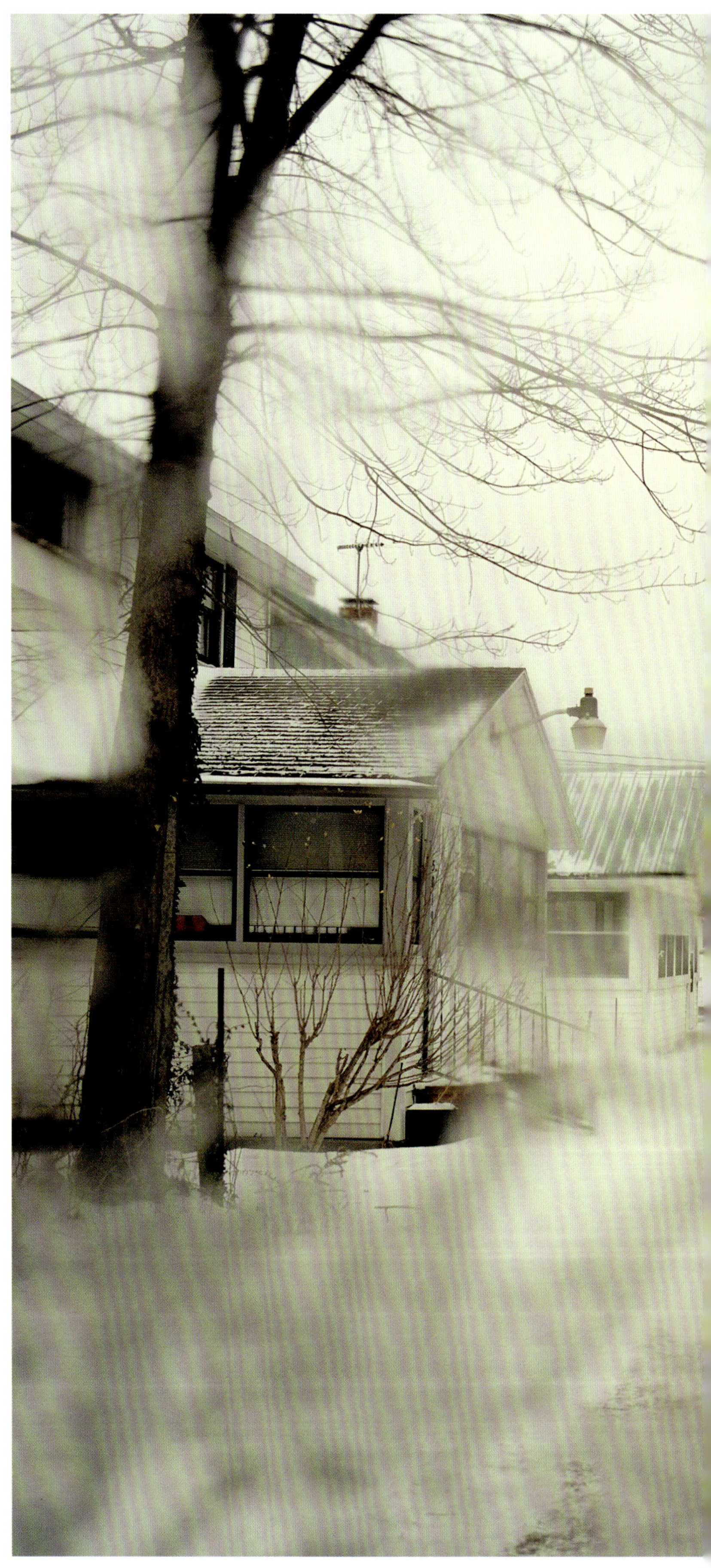

Todd Hido
#10106

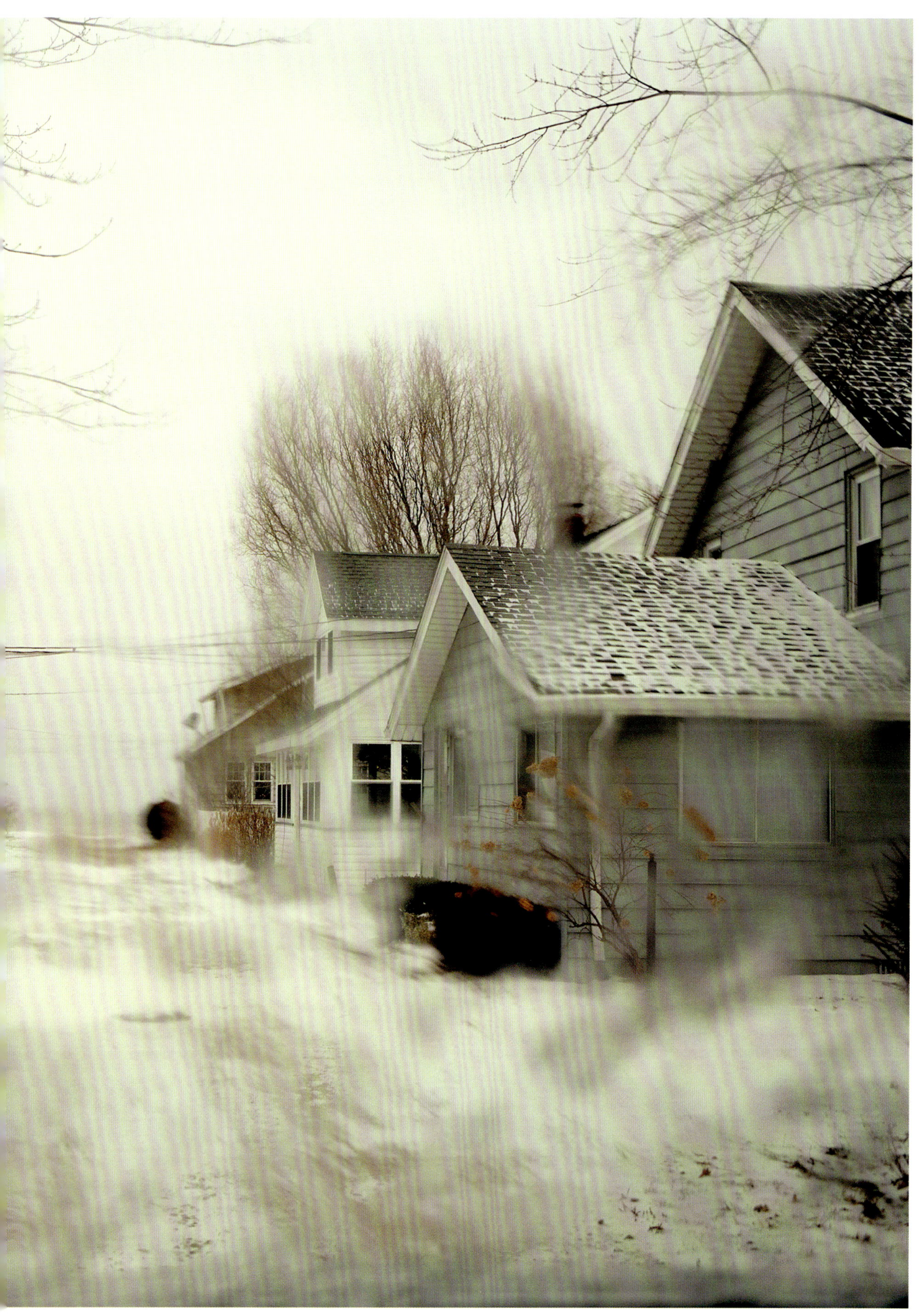

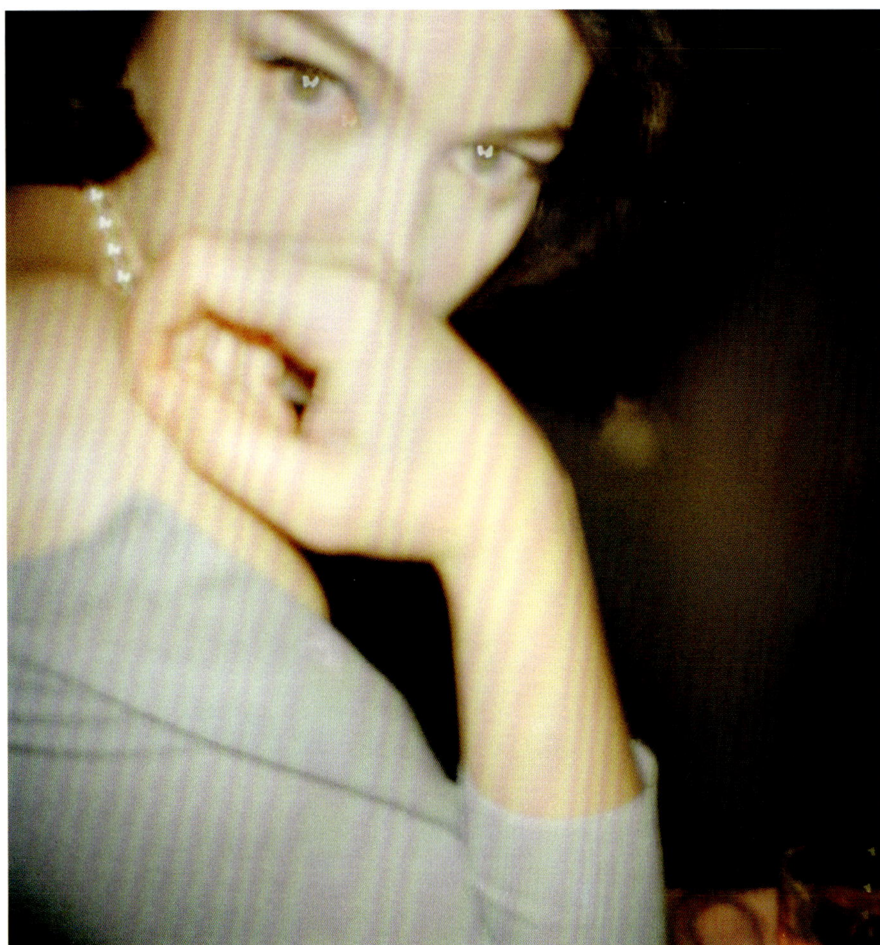

I used to tease Jim Goldberg about having so many different cameras. On one shoot, he might bring a video camera, two Polaroids, a 35 mm, a 4-by-5, and a medium-format camera. I'd say, "Jim, you have so many damn cameras. How do you even think?" Or, "The best shooters use one camera and use it really well." He'd reply, "It works fine for me."

I didn't get it then. I was a student, and he was more advanced than I was. If you're still learning your way around, you have to master one thing at a time, eliminate the variables, before you can branch out. Otherwise you're just wasting time. You find a film that works and you keep using it until you've mastered it. You find a lens that works and you continue to use it until you no longer have to think about it.

I wasn't ready for five cameras when I saw Jim working. Then, slowly but surely, it started to make sense to me. Sometimes now, I'll use two or three cameras. I understand why one would want to use multiple cameras, have a broader palette. Every camera makes a different kind of picture. Every camera is like a different paintbrush. They record scenes in different ways.

Sometimes I'll use a camera that creates a very subtle difference just for the effect. I have a camera where the flash drags a little bit, and it makes a

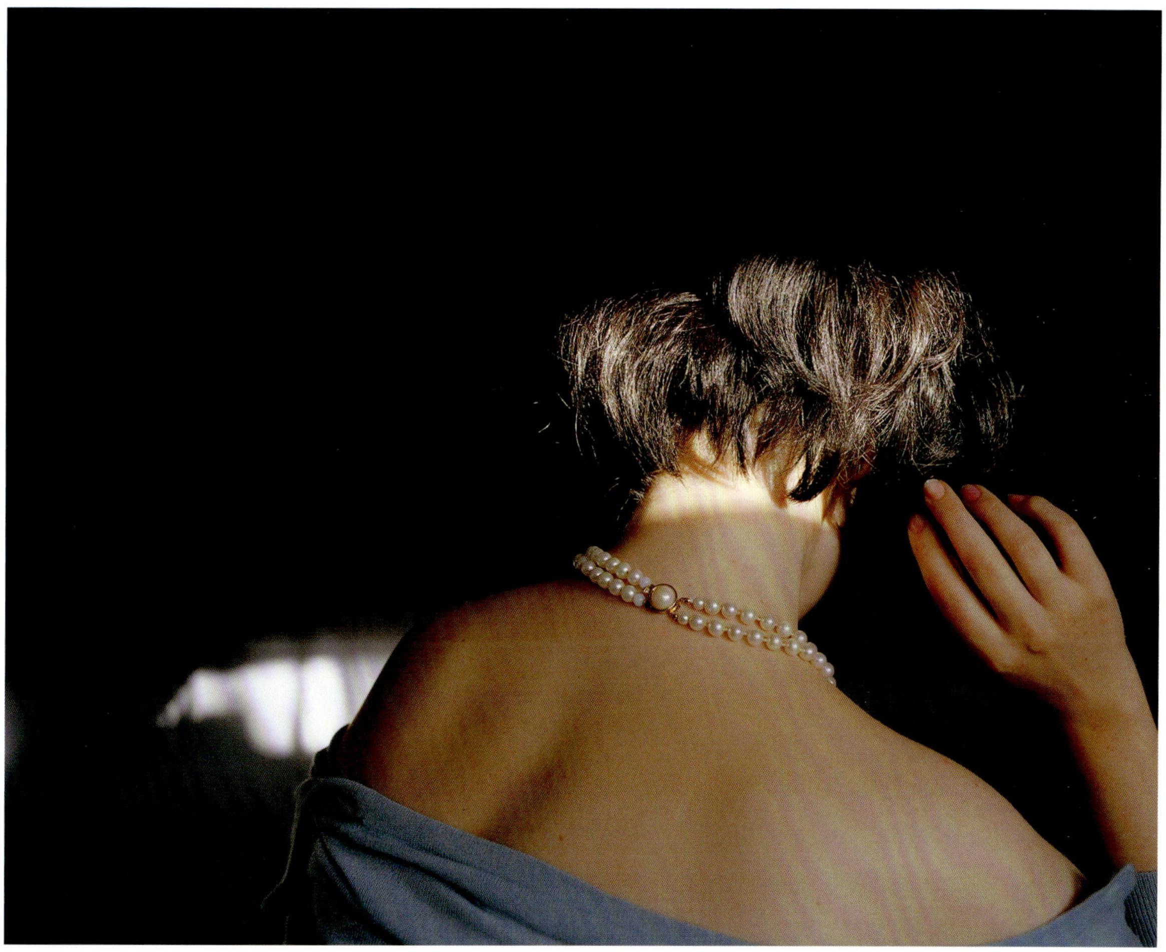

slightly blurred picture and creates a butterfly catchlight in the subject's eye. Because the camera is a little shaky, it produces photographs that seem like something urgent is happening.

When I bring all of the different pictures together from the different cameras, it's like looking at the same thing from multiple points of view. It adds up to more than me just taking a portrait of someone. It's like taking portraits as if they're made by different photographers.

I made these photographs of Khrystyna with three different cameras. I probably shot ten or fifteen frames on each camera, and each one made a completely unique kind of picture. I could tell the story through different views, and each one added something new to my understanding.

While it is the same scene taken with different cameras, the syntax of the whole thing is richer as if I were putting sentences together with words from different languages. One of the photos looks like the past. One of them looks like the present. Another could be a police picture. One could have been made by a fine art photographer, another, by an amateur. Yet another one could look like a painter made the picture.

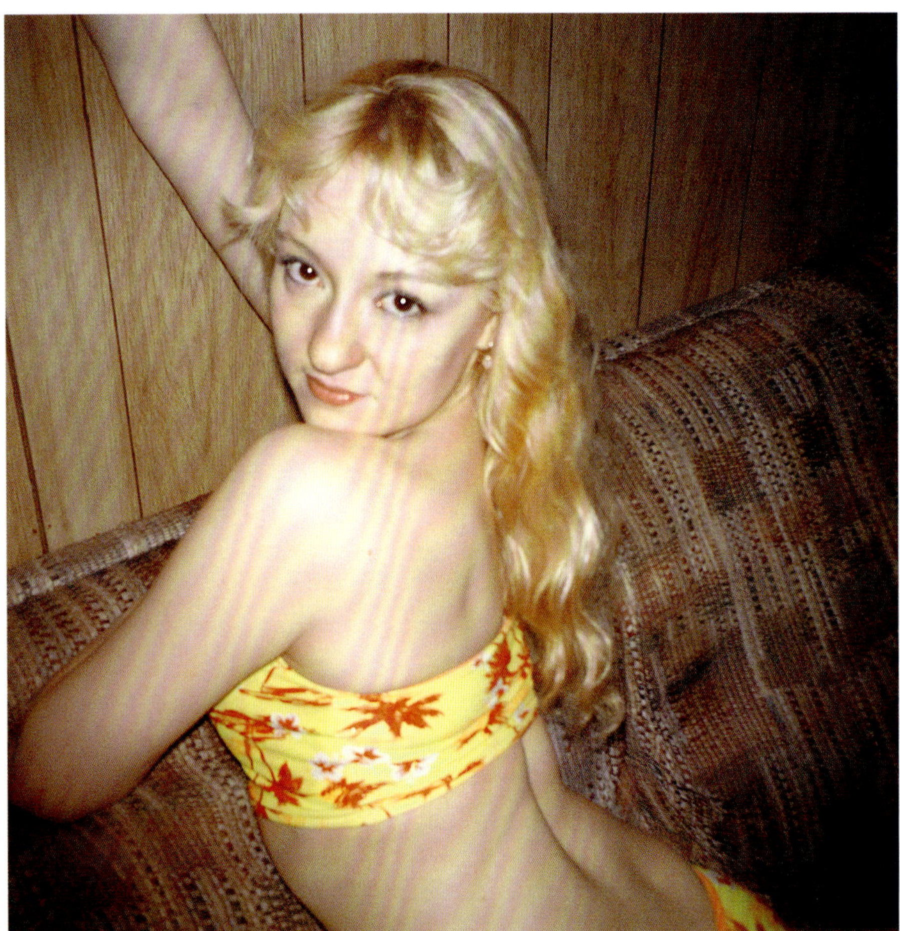

I started taking pictures with an Instamatic camera—the same camera I had as a kid. When I got the results back, I saw that the camera produced an entirely distinct look, an amateur snapshot look. I started using it in my portrait sessions.

I deliberately mimicked vernacular photography by using a camera that an amateur photographer would have used at home. Aside from it being really liberating to not photograph with a tripod, where everything is perfectly straight, the amateur quality of the images brings a particular feeling for the subject to the surface. The flash cuts through all the bullshit, right to their sad soul. Or my sad soul. Every portrait is a self-portrait.

Using multiple cameras and formats has added new layers of richness to my work. I also combine found photographs in with my own sometimes to broaden the story in a different way. When you put a male protagonist next to a portrait shot with an amateur camera, the viewer assumes he took it. I love that kind of twisting the story. I'm the narrator, but all of a sudden, someone else is the narrator.

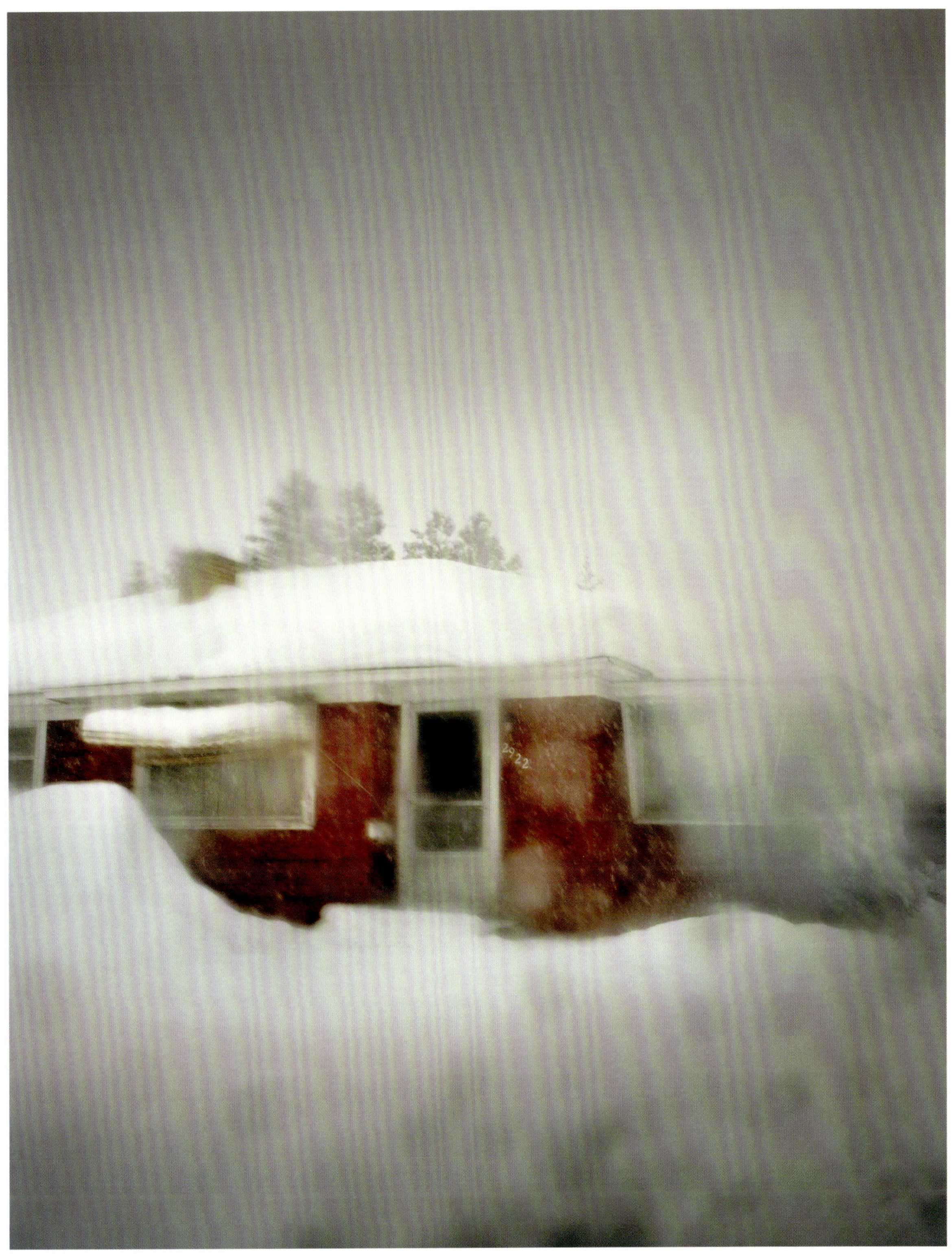

Todd Hido
#8610

Paper Movies

What I'm really talking about here is putting together picture sequences that will be collected together into a book. The book can lead you to synthesize ideas and can become your permanent record of a body of work. When you pick up a book, you expect something from it. It has a structure: a beginning, a middle, an end. It's an enclosed medium that you can come close to perfecting.

A lot of times, I'll just start by pairing individual photographs, keeping in mind that each image should become stronger out of coming together. And when you have a number of pairs, you start to pair the pairs. And then all of a sudden you have these chains of pictures that start to show the shape and structure of the story.

I find it really helpful to work with pictures on paper, little printouts that you can move around on a table or on a wall. I've never found a fabulous pairing or a great sequence on a computer screen. For me, things start happening when I work with physical objects. I've accidentally sequenced some really great and surprising pairs of pictures because I had the ability to move paper around. The pictures scatter in a way that you can't control or plan. You set a couple of photos down and realize they work together. As you start placing things together and they start to form chains, you can move whole sections. It's like making a paper movie.

When you're putting together photographs for a book, it's helpful to think of music. There may be motifs that appear and repeat themselves in different iterations in a long sequence. You can create a rhythm by being consistent from image to image and by paying attention to how the images hang together. But once you've established a pattern, once the rhythm becomes familiar, break it. The viewer should be led along and then surprised. Just when the viewer knows what's coming, do something different. When they've just seen a number of houses at night, introduce a landscape from the daytime. The reader will think, "Where'd this come from, and why is it so blurry?" That picture is there specifically to keep the reader engaged, to be the wrong picture at the right time. In a way, it contaminates the rhythm and spoils the sequence, but in just the right way.

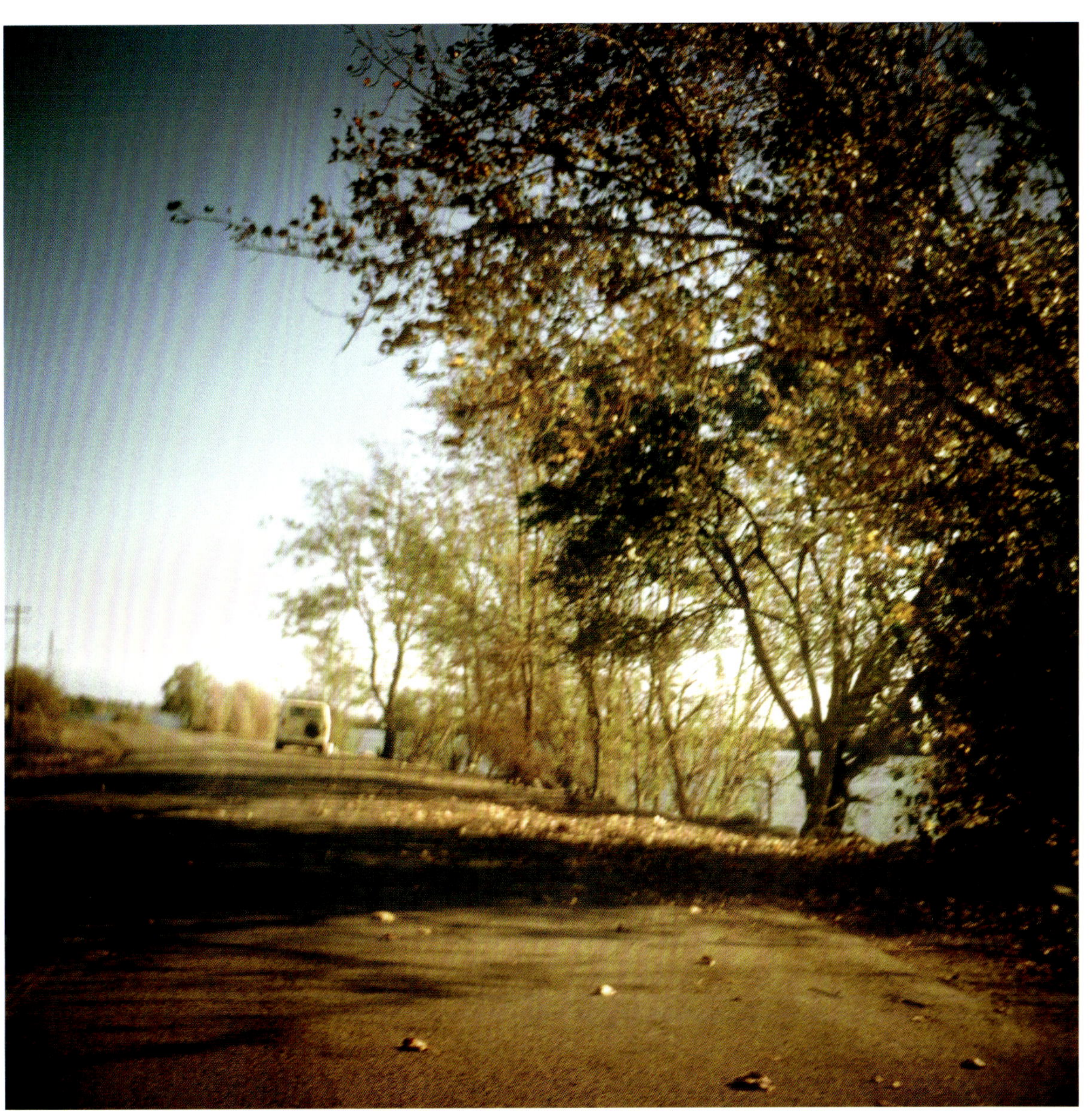

Todd Hido
#6017-a

115

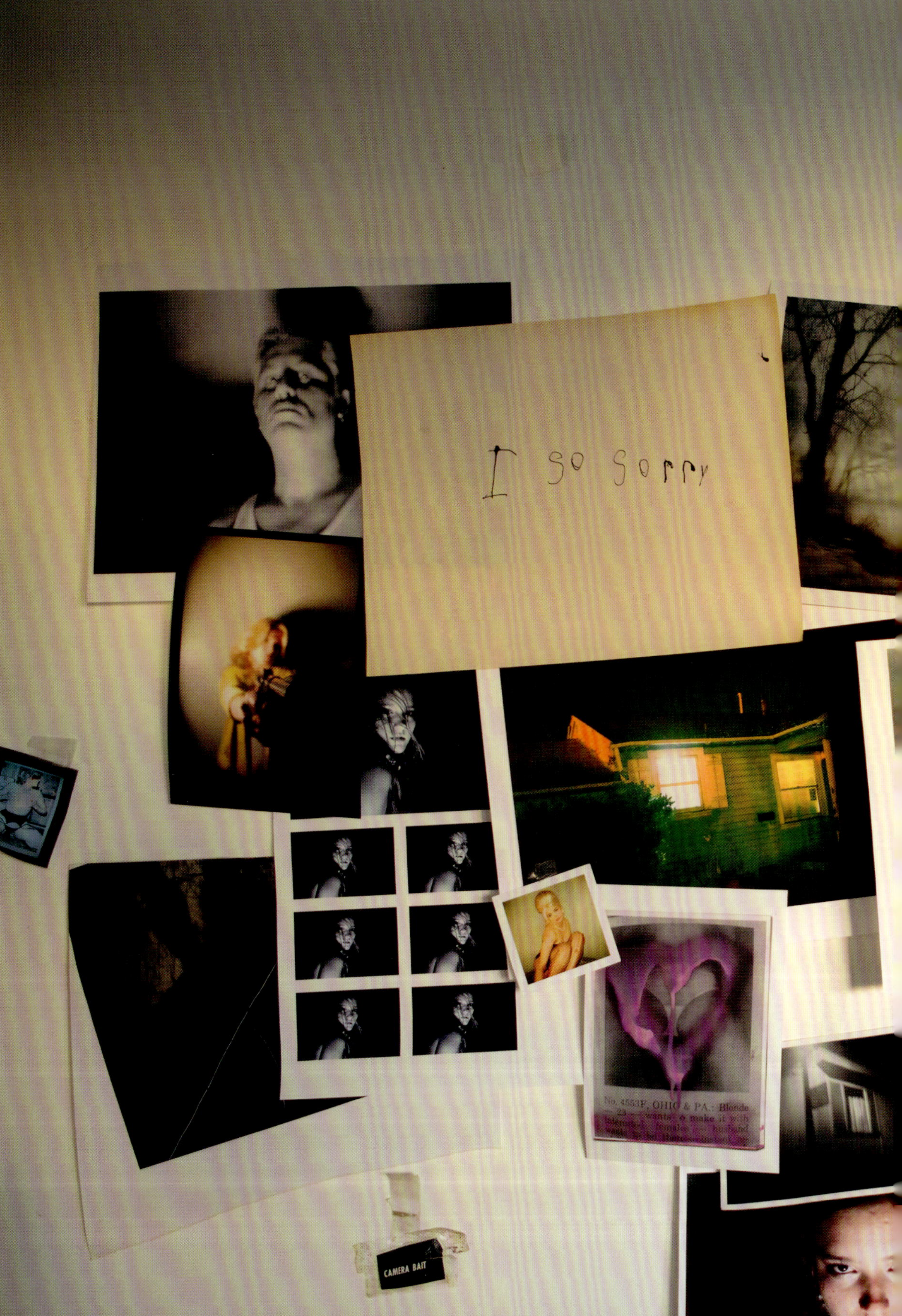

CAMERA BAIT
I so sorry
No. 4553F, OHIO & PA.: Blonde
CAMERA BAIT

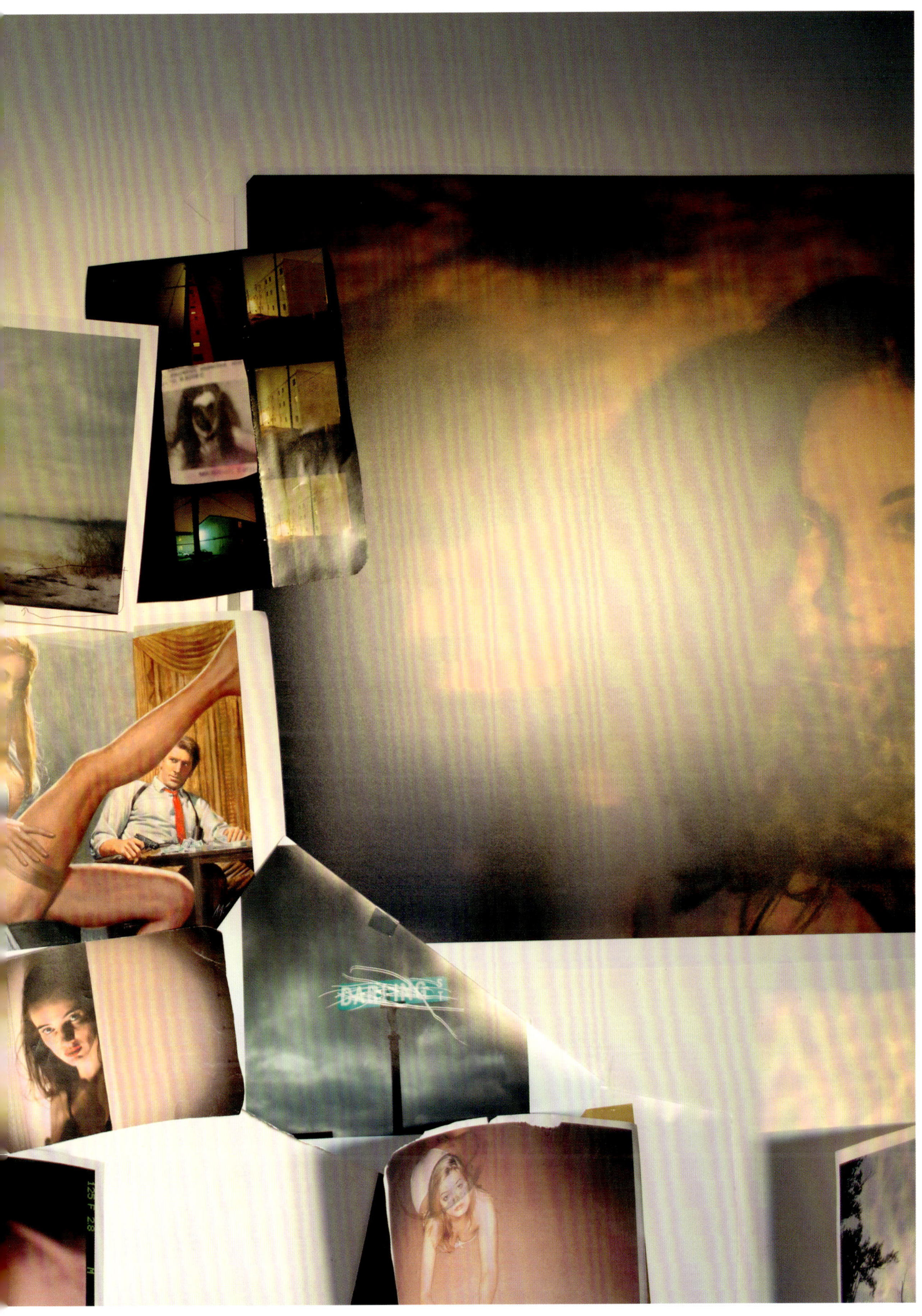

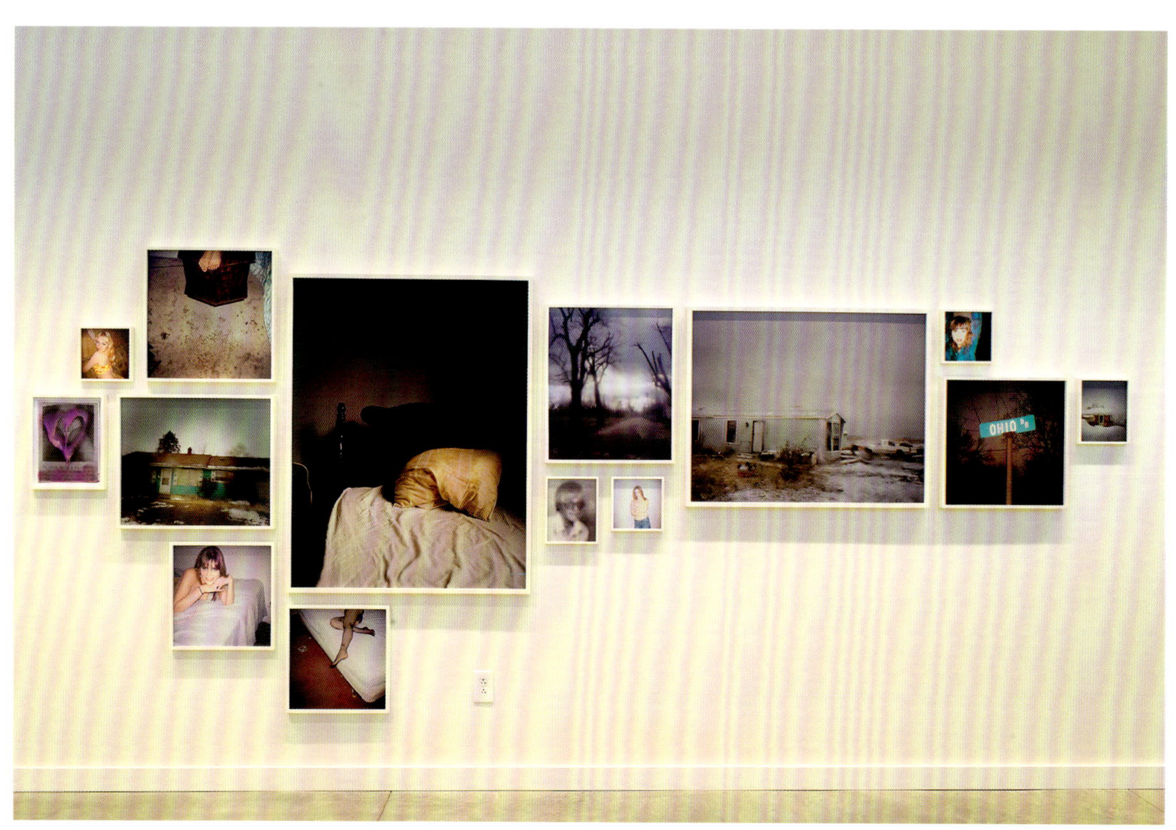

Turning Pages

Once you've made the paper movie, then you have to convert it into page-turning; there's nothing like page-turning. When I'm working on a book, I have to have a dummy. Simulating one on a computer is not acceptable. You have to print it and hold it in your hands.

You're making an object. Therefore, you have to bring it into the object world of paper and ink. Even if you make a rough dummy in black and white that is printed like crap and taped together with duct tape or whatever, you've got to be able turn the pages.

Making an object is crucial to photography. Everybody who is just shooting jpegs, they're in trouble. They've got to learn how to make an object, whether it's an image in a book or a print on the wall.

One thing I often see with young photographers is this rush to get their work out there. I'm very ambitious, but I also know that it's okay to wait until you're really ready to show a body of work. People have these different tabs on their website that show the portfolios of ten or fifteen projects. I don't have ten projects, and I'm twenty-five years into this. Sharing your work with the public is easier and quicker than ever—but just because you can, doesn't mean you should. Photographers also think that they need to have a book or a show right now. You don't. When the time is right, things will come together. In the meantime, try to enjoy making the pictures. Slow down and think about your craft.

Motivation and Inspiration

Once a book is printed and the show has come down, you have to stay motivated to go on to the next thing and make art on your own for the long haul. This is one of the biggest challenges for a working artist. There are all kinds of ways to get distracted. Like all of us, I've got stuff that I have to do most days that is not creative. You're not allowed to use the business of living or your job as an excuse to not make photographs.

Knowing what motivates you is key. Once you're out of school, you're on your own. There are no deadlines. No one's expecting work from you each week. You've got to figure out some method, whatever it is, that keeps you on track to make artwork. For some people, taking a class or meeting with a group on a regular basis is motivation enough. Some of us just need somebody to say, "Hey, I want to see what you're doing."

My friend Paul takes this introductory screen printing class every semester at a local community college. He's taken it so many times now that they eventually told him he couldn't sign up for it again. So now he signs up as Todd Hido, with my credit card—all so he can continue to take this class. The fact that every Wednesday he knows that he is supposed to go down there and screen print, is what keeps him working.

Something completely different might work for you. Everybody has to figure out how to survive after school—activities that get you out of that zone of being a drone.

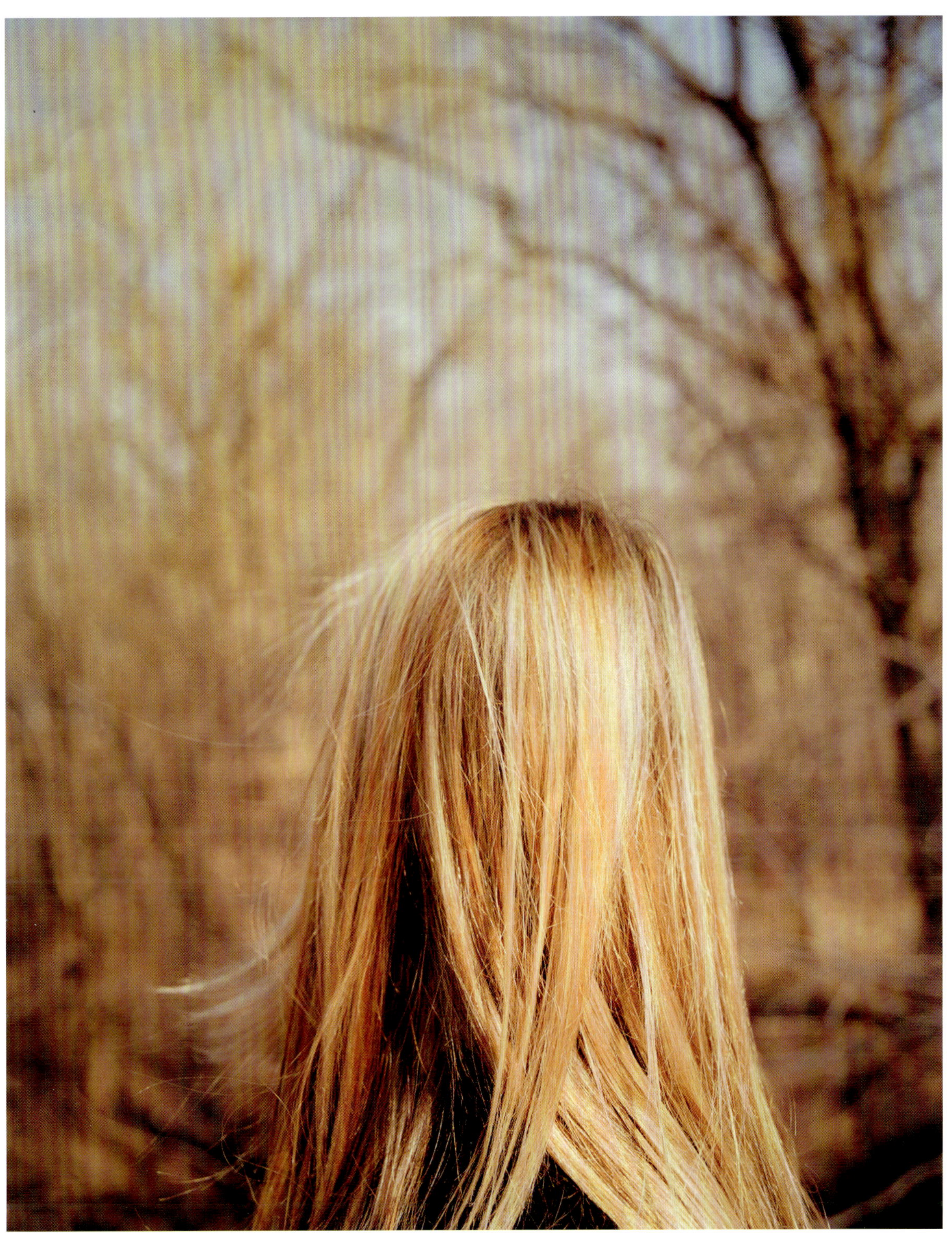

We all have a story to tell, and I believe that we can't help but tell it.

Some of us are bolder in the telling; others are more subtle. When you break it all down, there aren't an infinite number of things to photograph. One of the most remarkable documents I've ever seen was the shot list Roy Stryker made of the things he wanted the FSA photographers to shoot in order to convey the feeling of a common experience. He listed concrete ideas like, small towns, city, rural, industry, highways, weather—all with subheadings like, home in the evening, goods on shelves, vacant lots, car on the side of the road. The lists still apply today. These are the components of telling a story, of making a full body of work. If I ever run dry of ideas I'm going to look up those FSA shooting scripts for a lifetime's worth of inspiration.

Recommended Reading/Looking/ Listening

This list, from my 1996 thesis at the California College of the Arts, fueled me through graduate school and beyond.

— Todd Hido

Robert Adams. *Los Angeles Spring*. New York: Aperture, 1986.

Nobuyoshi Araki. *Femme de Mouche*. Tokyo: Mizuki, 1994.

Lewis Baltz. *Park City*. New York: Aperture, 1981.

Jean Baudrillard. *Cool Memories*. New York: Verso, 1987.

Bernd and Hilla Becher. *Water Towers*. Cambridge, Massachusetts: MIT Press, 1988.

Richard Billingham. *Ray's a Laugh*. Zurich and New York: Scalo, 1996.

Jeff Buckley. *Grace*. Columbia CK 57528, 1994, compact disc.

Italo Calvino. *Difficult Loves*. San Diego: Harcourt Brace Jovanovich, 1984.

Raymond Carver. *Short Cuts: Selected Stories*. New York: Vintage Books, 1993.

Larry Clark. *Teenage Lust*. New York: Larry Clark, 1987.

Walker Evans. *First and Last*. New York: Harper & Row, 1978.

Robert Frank. *Moving Out*. Authored by **Sarah Greenough**. Washington, D.C.: National Gallery of Art; Zurich and New York: Scalo, 1994.

Nan Goldin. *The Ballad of Sexual Dependency*. New York: Aperture, 1986.

Emmet Gowin. *Photographs*. New York: Alfred A. Knopf, 1976.

P. J. Harvey. *Rid of Me*. Island Records 314-514 696-2, 1993, compact disc.

Craigie Horsfield. *Craigie Horsfield*. Cambridge, Massachusetts: Cambridge Darkroom, 1988.

Edward T. Linenthal. *Preserving Memory: The Struggle to Create America's Holocaust Museum*. New York: Columbia University Press, 2001.

Liz Phair. *Exile in Guyville*. Matador OLE 051-1 2xLP, 1993, compact disc.

Richard Prince. *Girlfriends*. Rotterdam: Museum Boymans-van Beuningen, 1993.

Sophie Ristelhueber. *Aftermath: Kuwait, 1991*. London: Thames & Hudson, 1992.

Jo Spence and **Patricia Holland**. *Family Snaps: The Meanings of Domestic Photography*. London: Virago Press, 1991.

Larry Sultan. *Pictures from Home*. New York: Abrams, 1992.

Acknowledgments

First and foremost, to Denise Wolff, whom I met on a hot, Southern day in Virginia where we were both teaching a workshop. Sharing my knowledge of the medium is a pleasure for me, and I'm honored to be part of this book series.

To Darius Himes, for his support of my work in general and this book in particular.

To Robyn Taylor, whose work managing all the moving parts of this project kept it running. To Natalie Ivis, who helped behind the scenes on many of the details. To Schuyler Duffy, for organizing a productive workshop that kicked off the project. To Matt Harvey and Luke Chase, who worked diligently on the image reproductions.

To Greg Halpern, for writing a wonderful introduction to this book.

To Alexa Dilworth, for her help in polishing the text.

To Jena Shellito, for always keeping me focused on the priorities, and for helping me combat my tendency to do otherwise.

To Marina Luz, for her generous backup support when it got down to the wire.

And lastly, to all of my students, both past and present. I very much appreciate your enthusiasm and boundless curiosity, which energizes and inspires me. Your questions and even your dilemmas have enriched me along the way.

THE PHOTOGRAPHY WORKSHOP SERIES

Todd Hido

**on Landscapes, Interiors,
and the Nude**

Photographs and texts by Todd Hido
Introduction by Gregory Halpern

Front cover and flap (clockwise from top left): *#2690, #3225,
#10106, #1843, #6426*
Back cover (clockwise from top): *#8869, #2423-a, #1952*

Editor: Denise Wolff
Editorial Assistant: Robyn Taylor
Designer: Studio Rubic
Production: Matthew Harvey
Production Assistant: Luke Chase
Copy Editor: Alexa Dilworth
Proofreader: Madeline Coleman
Work Scholars: Natalie Ivis, Jessica Lancaster

The staff of the Aperture book program includes:
Chris Boot, Executive Director; Lesley A. Martin, Creative Director;
Taia Kwinter, Publishing Manager; Emily Patten, Publishing
Assistant; Susan Ciccotti, Senior Text Editor; Elena Goukassian,
Proofreader/Copy Editor; Samantha Marlow, Associate Editor;
Lanah Swindle, Editorial Assistant; Brian Berding, Designer;
Kellie McLaughlin, Director of Sales and Marketing; Richard Gregg,
Sales Director, Books

The Workshop Series is made possible, in part, with generous
support from S. B. Cooper and Rebecca Besson and the Besson/
Cooper Fund.

First edition, 2014
Printed in China
10 9 8 7 6

**Library of Congress Control
Number:** 2014944728
ISBN 978-1-59711-297-0

**To order Aperture books, or inquire
about gift or group orders, contact:**
+1 212.946.7154
orders@aperture.org

**For more information about Aperture
trade distribution worldwide, visit:**
aperture.org/distribution

aperture

Aperture Foundation
548 West 28th Street, 4th Floor
New York, NY 10001
aperture.org

Aperture, a not-for-profit foundation,
connects the photo community and
its audiences with the most inspiring
work, the sharpest ideas, and with each
other—in print, in person, and online.